P9-CBI-272

A Doctor's Guide to Erectile Dysfunction,

Any Man, Regardless of His Age or Medical History, Can Still Get an Erection

Dr. Kevin Hornsby, MD

Copyright©2012 by Dr. Kevin Hornsby

www.DrHornsbyMD.com

ISBN: 978-1-4675-0870-4

Printed and bound in the United States of America

DEDICATION

THIS BOOK IS DEDICATED TO Rick, a wise business partner, a mentor and a great friend. His intensity, focus, thoroughness and work ethic motivate and inspire me daily, sometimes pushing me to improve my areas of weakness. I am thankful that our paths crossed, knowing I am better for it. If it were not for his vision, this book would not exist. It was his initial idea, not mine.

I also depended on our clinic management staff to provide countless hours of effort bringing all the parts of this story into play. Their passion and devotion to what we do has fueled the movement we have made toward better and more successful outcomes in our offices every day for men suffering with erectile dysfunction.

Finally, this book is dedicated to Bill, a little energy ball of a man I shall never forget. Eighty-nine (89) years old, the last time I heard from him he was swimming 10 laps at the pool daily, enjoying sex every day with his young wife of 87, and had a mind as sharp as a laser. When I first met him, his first wife of 40 years had died suddenly and with no warning one cold night in an emergency room in central Florida. Emotionally devastated and impacted by years of health problems, he had not had a single erection in 10 years. He came to see me 2 days before he was to marry his new wife, whom he had met at his high school reunion. He left the office with a smile on his face and called me one week later to thank me. Bill is the embodiment of over 10,000 men and counting that I have had the privilege to help. Those men gave me a renewed confidence in the human spirit. Bill is a living example of our drive as human beings to live life to the fullest and to live it well until our very end.

ACKNOWEDGEMENTS

THE BOOK YOU HOLD IN your hands was born out of the efforts of a few dedicated very special people who shaped and cared deeply about my path in life. You should know about them. They saw something in a little sandy-haired, displaced small town boy in Alabama. I was rough hewn then, but they saw through to the future. They saw more. They saved me, polished me up, and made me shine.

It may come as a surprise to you, but no one acknowledged in this section was of highly-esteemed educated positions. They had no lofty goals in life, nor did they try to conquer the world; no medical awards hang on their office wall. These people breathed the life into this story, not I. With well-honed life skills, they coached the powerful precision analytical skills that I wield every day in the exam rooms of our offices. They guided me with a gentle hand at times, while at other's, they firmly called me to task—all the while shaping and molding me for this moment when I would meet you as you read these words.

Bernice Hornsby, a simple unassuming teacher I called my grandmother, died 30 years ago, but she was still the single most influential force behind the words that live in this book. She paced me through many days of my childhood, stoking a desire in me to learn. We studied painted turtle shells from the old bridge at the farm, and she pointed out differences in red-eared sliders and painted turtles. With the patience of Job, she explained things as I watched tadpoles morph into frogs—growing in a series of Ball mason jars she set up just for me at her kitchen window one summer. The thirst for knowledge she tended in me ultimately cultivated the medical cache of knowledge you'll find in this book. I'll never forget the night she woke me up at 2 a.m. to view a meteor shower. That simple passion seeded on the front porch of that old southern home grew into a passion and thirst for knowledge that propelled my path to the human anatomy labs at UAB medical school, to the Erectile Dysfunction Clinic and Urology rotations at UAB Hospital, and, ultimately, into our clinic exam rooms, where I may meet you some day. If I help you, it all started with a nurturing grandmother who saw more in me and planted a desire for learning.

Years later, after my grandmother died, Jerry Hughes noticed I didn't have enough money at school break. From that day forward, Jerry brought two dollars for lunch, one for him and one for me, equal and no difference. To this day, I have a deep and close relationship with him for what he did. Jerry changed the course of my life. Lawrence and Shirley, his parents, were unconditional, accepting me as a son and becoming cornerstones of my life. They lived out an example of helping others in front of me, sheltering over 30 foster children through the years after their start with me. Lawrence once drove a hitchhiker two hours extra to the bus station in Montgomery. The treatment ideas, tough medical cases, and moving stories of the patients that you will read came to life only because of the examples I emulated from these rare and fine people. Hard work, completing tasks, team work, doing something right, compassion for others, and the value of a quality of life were the gifts they imparted to me.

One summer, Lawrence refused to move the tractor to plow the tomatoes until the hatchling birds left the nest the mother bluebird built in the radiator. He embodied compassion—compassion I still mimic in the exam room with every patient. You will feel Lawrence's compassion in the pages of this book. Jerry Hughes impacted more men's lives than he would ever have imagined the day he drove up in that old Torino and carried me back to be part of their family—a starting point which stabilized me.

The finest medical degree is nothing but paper if its owner can't articulate his thoughts to the patient. My dad gave me the priceless gift of communication and ability to relate to patients. An ability never to be gleaned from a medical text book—like many of us do—it took both years and his death for me to fully understand the powerful, unique gift Dad gave me. He was a marketer-earthy, charming, and brilliant in sales (still to this day only rivaled by my partner, Rick). His massive impact influences much of my practice daily.

Never as a choice, but sometimes demanded by the practice of medicine, my family many times paid a heavy price in missed meals, Sunday night flights out, solo baseball practices, short notice schedule changes, and late nights with my head buried in a book to help a patient. The real unsung support cast, they provided safe, peaceful, and loyal companionship. Self sacrificing, they have always been there for me, tolerating unpredictable schedules and interrupted family activities. The story you are about to read provides the words, but my family provided the canvas and painted the story to my life.

These few, through their devotion to me, will impact many. My journey to this point has ridden on their shoulders. These remarkable people are rare in this world today. They served as living examples of the powerful force of helping just one person and the resulting positive ripple effect that can happen.

Enjoy your reading. I hope your life is changed for the better. I also hope to meet you sometime soon.

TABLE OF CONTENTS

INTRODUCTION

A Rewarding Sex Life Should be an Experience,
Not a Memory

MOST OF THE MEN WHO are reading this book never dreamed that they would need to. The majority has a history of a healthy and active sex life, but age, medical conditions and illnesses, and even family or lifestyle changes have affected their ability to perform or enjoy sexual intimacy with their partner. Suddenly, they find themselves in unfamiliar territory, one which they believe holds limited options and carries a preconceived stigma that results in a reluctance to seek support or medical treatment.

More than a decade ago, I never dreamed that I'd write this book, either. The path I'd charted for my life and career didn't include specializing in male sexuality and performance. I was interested in science and set out to obtain a degree in Zoology before realizing that I was better suited in a field that involved people, not animals. My longing for human interaction resulted in a change of direction as I set my sights on becoming a surgical assistant. It was during my residency that I was introduced to what became my true calling—a passion for helping men who suffer with the medical, emotional, and sexual effects of erectile dysfunction and premature ejaculation.

As a physician, I know that obtaining an accurate background and history is vital in the doctor-patient relationship. But I also know that the nature of my specialty requires a personal and intimate man-to-man conversation—one that is comfortable, open, and honest. That's why I believe it's just as important that my patients know my background and history as it is that I know theirs.

It comes as a surprise to many of my patients that I'm a lot like them. I have a great deal in common with the majority of them, in fact. Growing up in Dothan, a small town in southeast Alabama, I was raised by my grandmother. I credit her with instilling in me the love for science that led me to the medical profession. At the young age of 12, though, my grandmother passed away, and I was placed in foster care.

My foster family were construction workers—roofers by trade. They taught me how to roof and how to plant a crop and reap the harvest on their farm. I took those hard-working traits with me when I went to college at Auburn

University, where I worked my way through school by loading trucks for the men in brown at UPS. At one point, I even sold pencils. Every dime counted and every job became another life experience that molded the person I am today.

When I changed my major from zoology to medicine, I transferred to the University of Alabama Medical School, where I trained in an Erectile Dysfunction Clinic, conducting clinical trials while in medical residency. What I thought was a necessary means to becoming a surgical assistant became a lifelong passion. At the time, I wasn't aware of the importance of the clinical trials we conducted, but because I understood the very real need for it, I became fascinated with finding treatments and cures for the men who suffer, usually in silence, with erectile dysfunction. Knowing that this was one place where I could make a difference, where I could actually change lives, I entered an uncommon specialty which treats an underserved population.

Some of the same medicines we used in clinical trials during my residency are used to treat men today, but the options have grown tremendously. With different combinations and dosages, there are now 160 different options available for men, even if they have a history of hypertension, diabetes, cancer, or a wide array of other medical problems. The precise formula and dosage are unique for each individual, but the results are almost always favorable. In fact, the majority of our patients see immediate results during their very first visit.

Whether our patients are 27 or 97—yes, 97—we've been able to help them regain their lost sex life, ignite stagnant relationships, and rebuild their confidence and self-esteem, not only in bed, but in all areas of their lives. We believe that men of any age can have a satisfying sex life. We also wholeheartedly believe that men should never have to suffer in silence, fearful or embarrassed to seek help in obtaining a healthy and active sex life—it's as natural and basic as eating and drinking to our physical and emotional well-being.

That's precisely why I chose my specialty, and it's also why I wrote this book. I believe every man deserves to be sexually active for his entire life. In this book, you'll learn about many of them, including men who had prostate cancer and other medical issues, hormonal imbalances, life changes, and performance insecurities. They're men just like you, who stepped forward out of their silence and sought treatment because they didn't want to live the rest of their life in celibacy. I hope that through their stories and the information revealed in this book, men everywhere will be inspired to join the thousands of patients I've successfully helped to regain sexual function. They're a testament to men everywhere that a satisfying sex life doesn't have to come with an expiration date.

THE PROBLEMS

Chapter One

SILENT SUFFERERS

I CONSIDER MYSELF FORTUNATE TO be one of the few who embarked on a career path that has become more rewarding and fascinating throughout the years. What began as a medical residency has turned into a personal and professional mission to improve the quality of life for my patients. It's sad, but true, that I cannot help every man who suffers from erectile dysfunction or premature ejaculation, though. But that's not because there is no help for them—it's because they don't seek help for a condition which is very treatable.

When a patient walks through my doors, I find that I'm often their last resort. They've already tried Viagra®, Levitra®, or Cialis® (sometimes all three), and were disappointed to discover that they don't always work. For some, they did work, but the side effects of those drugs outweighed the benefits. Some of my patients have also tried external pumps, only to find that the devices were painful, countering the effect that they were seeking.

Then they're back at square one, where they often resign themselves to a sexless life because they don't know where to turn...or embarrassment leaves them reluctant to explore other options.

I've witnessed the overwhelming devastation of self-esteem and relationships caused by sexual dysfunction. Yet, too many men adopt a sense of shame about their condition, and it's that shame that keeps them from seeking medical treatment that does work. It's the stigma of silence that I encounter every day in my practice that I'm aiming to erase. Erectile dysfunction is nothing to be ashamed of—in fact, most of the time, it's not attributed to an individual's sexuality or masculinity. The majority of cases of erectile dysfunction are caused by medical conditions.

Women don't always understand a man's reluctance to get help when they encounter sexual problems. There is a line between men and women, and it's called communication. Women are far better communicators; men, on the other hand, are better silent sufferers.

There is a psychological component to these issues that goes far beyond the difference between men and women. A man's sexuality and the ability to perform directly impact his self-esteem. I've witnessed it in thousands of patients, who walk in to my office down and defeated. They feel like they've failed, and over the years, that feeling supersedes everything that is good about them. It invades their relationships, the performance at work, their confidence, their stress levels, and above all, their ability to be happy. My job is to reverse that psychological component and the male tendency to accept their condition and the prospect of an unfulfilling and sexless life.

First, I want men and women to know that almost every man has suffered from erectile dysfunction or premature ejaculation at some point in their lives. It might be due to stress in another area of their life, pressure to perform, or over excitement. But it can also be attributed to the number one cause for erectile dysfunction—medical conditions, like prostate cancer.

With a higher demographic of baby boomers who have now reached the age of 50, we're seeing an increasing number of men who have had prostate surgery. My foster father was one of them. One of the reasons behind this increase is that the medical community now recommends screening at an earlier age. New guidelines recommend that black males have a prostate screening as early as age 45 and that white males be checked at the age of 50. Early screenings save lives, but they also result in more prostate surgeries, which in turn, results in a higher number of men with the side effects of those surgeries—erectile dysfunction being one of them.

There is good news, though. Modern day prostate surgery is less invasive than it was in the past. Only ten years ago, radical prostatectomies were performed, often with little regard to the nerves. Today, however, patients enjoy the benefits of nerve-sparing procedures, which are less likely to cause erection problems. Still, despite efforts to minimize damage to the nerves in the surrounding area, 80 percent of men experience some type of erection problem after prostate surgery.

Diabetes and metabolic syndrome are also sexual culprits for many of my patients. Most diabetics are aware that the disease causes damage to nerve endings in the body, but they don't realize that the nerve endings in the penis are also affected. I've had many patients with diabetes who came to me, complaining that they couldn't get an erection—they couldn't ejaculate or climax. In fact, some had lost all feeling in their penis—their nerve endings were that severely damaged. One man even admitted that even though he couldn't feel any sensation in his penis, he still wanted to be able to get an erection, for his partner's sake. We were able to accomplish that, giving both him and his partner what they wanted.

That is why I am so very passionate about what I do. Of the thousands of men I've treated, too many are initially embarrassed and ashamed to admit that they need help. They're not aware that erectile dysfunction isn't an indication that they're less of a man. In fact, after I make a diagnosis based on their medical and sexual history, they're usually surprised and relieved to find that a medical problem is to blame. It's more than rewarding to witness them transform from being embarrassed to admit they have a problem, to being ecstatic that they're able to experience a long overdue erection—all in the same appointment.

Medicine is an amazing vehicle—it's a science and an art. Yet, finding the right solution, in the right combinations, for each patient is not entirely a science. It's a process that requires open, full communication between doctor and patient. In other words, we must remove the stigma of shame that results in silence. There is no such thing as too much information in my field. Full disclosure is usually the key to finding a solution. That's true whether you're a young, vibrant athlete who suffers from premature ejaculation or an 80-year-old man who still wants to enjoy sex with his wife of 50-plus years. I've successfully treated men at both ends of that spectrum, and each time, I'm rewarded as I watch their transformation. In this book, you'll learn about some of them. They're guys just like you—single, married, divorced, and widowed. They're fresh out of college and decades past retirement. They're colonels and chartered boat captains. They've conquered the world, and now they're committed to conquering their problems in the bedroom.

I'm committed to helping every last one of them.

Chapter Two

ERECTILE DYSFUNCTION

WHAT IS ERECTILE DYSFUNCTION, AND why is it happening to me? Do you whisper when you ask that question, or do you prefer to silently run it through your mind, over and over, only to find that a logical answer isn't forthcoming? If so, you're like the majority of my patients, who tend to "wait it out," hoping that their problems will miraculously go away, as suddenly as they appeared.

While erectile dysfunction can happen suddenly, seemingly overnight, it's usually a gradual process that men mistakenly attribute to aging. That's unfortunate, though, because while aging can be blamed for hair loss, wrinkles, and metabolic changes in the body, it's not necessarily a factor in sexual desire or ability to perform. I've successfully treated couples well into their 80's who will attest to that fact.

Like I've previously said, sexual dysfunction is often

not a diagnosis—it's a symptom of another problem. Erectile dysfunction and premature ejaculation are usually caused by other physical or psychological issues which impact a man's sexual performance. Let's take a look at the condition, the causes, and the various solutions.

WHAT IS ERECTILE DYSFUNCTION?

Some people refer to erectile dysfunction (ED) as impotence. Regardless of the name, erectile dysfunction isn't the same as a lack of sexual desire, and it's completely different from premature ejaculation, which we'll cover in later chapters. Erectile dysfunction is the partial or complete inability to achieve an erection or to sustain one that is suitable for intercourse. This could mean a complete inability to become erect, or it could refer to the inability to maintain an erection long enough to have sex. While erectile dysfunction is a diagnosis, it is also a symptom—one which is usually the result of a medical problem or a psychological problem.

To properly explain what erectile dysfunction really is, it's necessary to understand what causes an erection and how it occurs.

All erections are not the same. Erections are as individual and unique as the man who has them. They are inconsistent, sometimes needing more stimulation, sometimes less. They vary in degrees of firmness and length of time.

An erection occurs when the brain receives a signal that stimulation has occurred. The brain responds by sending out other signals, telling the muscles that surround arteries to loosen or relax, thus allowing increased blood flow to enter those areas. That blood flow happens quickly, and when it reaches capacity, the penis swells and becomes firm and an erection takes place. The erection is sustained because of the pressure against the skin and will continue as long as the brain continues to send signals. Even during this process, though, there can be varying degrees of intensity and firmness, increasing and decreasing from time to time.

When do erections occur? They can occur at any time of the day or night. They can also occur at any age. Surprising to some, male infants in the womb have erections, and so do men in their 80's and 90's. Of course, these are not all the direct result of sexual stimulation—proof that not all erections are the product of lust or sexual interest. They are rather simply a natural part of a healthy male's reproductive system.

It should be noted that in a healthy male, erections can occur when they are willed, and when they are not wanted. One good example is nocturnal erections, which occur when men dream. It's a myth that men are dreaming about sex when they wake up with an erection. Yes, these nocturnal erections are the result of a dream, but that dream can be about anything. The fact of the matter is that any dream produces an erection in a healthy male. When a man wakes up with an erection, a common scenario, he has most likely been awakened during or just after having a dream. Arousal is not a necessary contributing factor. This is one reason why physicians inquire whether a man suffering from ED has morning erections. It helps us identify whether the condition is physical or the result of a psychological factor, such as stress.

The length of time a man is able to maintain an erection is individual. There is no set time span that determines what is "normal" or what is considered to be healthy. Basically, if a man is able to become erect and hold an erection long enough to satisfactorily engage in intercourse, medical intervention is usually not warranted or necessary.

Erectile dysfunction occurs when a male cannot achieve an erection or sustain it long enough for sexual activity and ejaculation. As I've previously noted, occasional or temporary impotence occurs in nearly all males at some time in their lives. At one time, it was the public and medical perception that psychological factors were to blame for nearly all incidents of erectile dysfunction. However, modern medicine has taken us into the 21st century, where we now know that the majority of ED cases are the result of physical or medical problems. Certainly, there are some cases which can be related to psychological factors or a combination of medical and psychological factors.

Regardless of the cause, though, it is apparent that erectile dysfunction stemming from any origin affects men psychologically.

WHO IS AFFLICTED WITH ERECTILE DYSFUNCTION?

ED is common among men; most men suffer from occasional, temporary, or short-term ED at some point in their lives. However, five percent of males aged 40 and higher and as much as 20 to 25 percent of men 65 and older have long-term erectile dysfunction.

I should point out, though, that erectile dysfunction can strike any man at any age. Most people mistakenly believe that it's an "old man" condition, but I can assure you that, even though it is less frequent, it can occur to young men, as well—men in their twenties or thirties. It's a non-discriminating condition that strikes even the most sexually active males.

Television shows have turned to ED as entertainment material. Remember Sam, the "studly" bartender on the sit-com *Cheers?* Sam prided himself on his sexual prowess and ability to please women, so when he found that he was unable to perform in one episode, he was devastated. Other TV shows have made light of ED, and it certainly has been the subject of many a joke. But when it strikes in reality and in the bedroom, the laughter subsides and is replaced with a sense of fear, embarrassment, and a loss of self-esteem.

When do you need to see a doctor? Usually, there is nothing to worry about if you're having a temporary problem, especially if you've been ill or are undergoing major life changes. You should consult with a specialist, though, if you're unable to achieve or sustain an erection 50 percent of the time or more. In that instance, it's likely that there are underlying problems which require medical intervention.

Problems with erections may stem from medications, chronic illnesses, poor blood flow to the penis, drinking too much alcohol, scar tissue, psychological reasons, or being too tired. Lifestyle changes, medications, and other treatments are often used to treat ED. While the treatment is a science, it's also based on personal, as well as medical factors, and it relies heavily on the communication between doctor and patient.

For example, Andy's 25 years old. He's in a relationship, but is becoming confused, unsure if he's ready for the level of commitment that a serious, long-term relationship will require. Over the course of a few weeks, his sexual desire wanes. Eventually, he's surprised to find that his healthy sexual performance has been halted due to erectile dysfunction.

Then, there's Joe. Joe is 49, married, and has recently joined the ranks of the unemployed. He, too, finds himself suffering from an unprecedented inability to achieve an erection suitable for sexual activity.

Neither Andy nor Joe has any medical problems, per se, outside of their recent ED symptoms. Neither knows what to do about it. When these two gentlemen seek treatment, the physician will request a thorough medical and personal background, which will hopefully reveal the strains and stresses they're undergoing. In this example, reducing their stress will most likely provide the cure. But, they may need help in overcoming their stress. They could receive the same treatment, but it's just as likely, if not more, that they'll receive different treatments. That could be because of their age, the varying reasons behind their performance problems, or because every body responds differently to the treatments available. What works for one man is not certain to work for another, a fact proven time and again with the patients I've treated, and one which is more evident in the following correlation.

Ken and John are both 62 years old. They both have a wife, children, and grandchildren. They are of relatively similar height and weight, and they even live in the same town. Medically, they've been relatively healthy all of their lives, until last year, when they both had prostate surgery. Now, they are both suffering from post-surgical ED. Ken and John could receive the exact same treatment and respond identically to it—or they could very well each require a totally different combination of drugs and/or therapies. Either way, it should be noted that the ED condition they're both currently suffering is treatable.

Because of the vast and diverse causes of erectile dysfunction, the wide age variances, lifestyles, and medical histories of the patients who suffer from it, I believe it will be helpful to discuss the causes of ED, as well as the treatments and what they entail. While this list might not be all inclusive, it does cover the most common and prevalent causes of erectile dysfunction and the common, as well as innovative, treatments available to physicians to provide their patients, and even future trends and research which might provide even more effective options.

I hope that this information and the case studies which support them will serve to reassure all men that there is hope and treatment for ED, regardless of the cause, how long it has affected their lives, their age, or their medical history. The solution every man who suffers from erectile dysfunction is seeking is available, and my goal is to make sure that each of them is able to enjoy a healthy and active sexual life. It is no longer necessary to suffer in silence.

STRESS AND OTHER PSYCHOLOGICAL CAUSES OF ED

Boredom: A man's sexual desire is fueled by stimuli—taste, touch, smell, sight, and yes, even sound. When that stimuli is missing, it's not unusual that he will experience a lack of response, as well. A man's erection is often the result of direct stimulation or desire that stems from an outside source. When the stimulating trigger or desire is removed, it can result in waning sexual desire. Boredom sets in without stimulation, as well. When an otherwise healthy sexual desire and ability to become erect lessen, couples can bring it back by providing new, different and exciting stimulation.

The first time you had sex, it was a new and exciting experience. You might have been nervous or overly excited, but you can probably admit that you weren't bored. The stimulation was there. But as in so many things, when you do something over and over again, the very same way, in the very same place, at the very same time, it becomes less exciting and more of a routine. Yes, even sex can become routine and cause you to fall into a rut. In that case, try being creative. Add music to the scene and create a seductive atmosphere. Divert from your usual foreplay. Instigate sex at unusual times and in different places. Talk about what you like and what you want. Oftentimes, when the stimulation returns, so does the excitement and the resulting erection.

PRESSURE TO PERFORM

Another common precursor to the ability to become erect is pressure, particularly the pressure to perform. Performance anxiety disorder symptoms can include the inability to get a penile erection or the loss of an erection before or during sex. Why does performance anxiety impact men to this degree? One reason is because it places all responsibility for intercourse on the male, and in some cases, the male puts all responsibility on himself for the quality of the sex.

One of the most common times when pressure to perform strikes is when a couple is attempting to conceive a child. In that case, the pressure is two-fold: one, the male must perform for conception to take place; and two, the male carries a great deal of the weight on his shoulders that has performed sufficiently to impregnate his partner. Let's not forget, though, the major contributing factor that increases this pressure—the man has to perform in a specific window of time, and often repeatedly during that time.

What happens here? The pleasure that's usually obtained from sex can be missing. Stress sets in as desire wanes, and sex becomes a chore. It's not uncommon and usually fixes itself once conception takes place or sex occurs at a different time of the month, when the pressure isn't a factor. However, for the couple who is having difficulty to conceive, it naturally can pose a problem. In this case, reintroducing excitement into the sex life can help the male forget the pressures of the moment. Relaxing and lessening the pressure to perform also can enhance performance. That's why we hear many stories of couples who have not been able to conceive for long periods of time, and then, after giving up, find themselves unexpectedly pregnant.

Performance anxiety can also occur with new partners. A desire to satisfy a woman in bed, especially the first time, can place tremendous stress on a man. Talking and taking it slowly can reduce the anxiety. Some men also find it helpful if they try not to think about climaxing or the need to bring their partner to orgasm.

One of the most memorable and remarkable cases of performance anxiety was presented to me about a year ago. A gentleman came to our clinic and shared a touching personal history. This man had been married for 20 years. He had a marriage that was rare. Over the course of two decades, their sexual desire never waned. In fact, he and his wife wanted and had sex twice a day, every day for 20 years. That's proof that men can be satisfied in a long-term monogamous relationship. His marriage was indeed a successful and happy one, but it took a tragic turn when his wife died suddenly in the middle of the night. He was so emotionally traumatized by her death that he didn't have an erection for the next ten years, *ten years!* It's difficult to grasp such a life change, going from twice-daily sex every day to absolutely nothing. He went from sex at the frequency of a rabbit to total celibacy, proving that the influence of the human mind is a very powerful thing. After ten years of celibacy, he came to me. He had reunited with his old high school sweetheart and wanted to regain his sexual performance, but he needed help. As I listened to his story, I was deeply touched by his feelings for both of the women in his life—his wife whom he still obviously loved and his new romantic interest, whom he just as obviously wanted to enjoy being with. I treated this gentleman, and his sex life resumed. For the first time in ten years, he was able to enjoy something that had brought him so much daily pleasure for most of his adult life.

Examples like this show how important performance is to man and how devastating it is to lose it. I see the pain that's caused from erectile dysfunction. I also see the embarrassment and the humiliation. I go to work every day hoping that I can relieve that pain, embarrassment, and humiliation for every patient that walks through the door. While every patient doesn't share the story of the man who had sex twice a day for 20 years and abruptly went to nothing, the varying degrees of performance anxiety and erectile dysfunction they do have can affect them just as profoundly. For many, the inability to maintain an erection is just as painful as the inability to achieve an erection.

Erectile dysfunction also includes the loss of an erection and the inability to regain it. This can result from the pressure to perform or from being overly anxious. In this instance, time often produces a cure, but for some men, it's a common problem. There are multiple reasons, none of which are uncommon. Here are a few of their stories:

Jake, 29, has no trouble getting an erection, but finds that he loses it just before intercourse, almost always when he pauses to put on a condom.

In this case, the distraction is probably the culprit. If Jake is able to self stimulate or maintain an erection when not using a condom, he might benefit by using different ways to stimulate and keep his excitement from waning long enough to get past this interruption. However, if this is a continual pattern, Jake could benefit from treatment that would prevent this from occurring in the future.

Ross is in the final stages of a divorce. He's in his mid 40's and has custody of their two children—both pre-teens. He hasn't had sex in almost two years. However, during that time, he has been able to successfully masturbate. A new romantic interest enters Ross' life, and for the very first time, he cannot sustain an erection long enough to make love to her. In Ross' own words, he's scared and embarrassed.

Whoa! Ross certainly has a lot of change going on in his life, and with it, a lot of stress and pressure. Significant life changes, like divorce or new partners, can create havoc on our emotions and dump a truckload of anxiety, guilt, and even over excitement on the ability to perform. Ross could very well be suffering from performance anxiety disorder, which does happen when a man switches partners. Being scared only adds to the stress he's already feeling. It's a well-known fact that stress can cause physical problems. My first piece of advice to Ross is to have a thorough check-up examination to make sure there aren't any physical problems causing his performance. Once that is ruled out, he should seek treatment for what is probably a temporary problem.

As you can see, each of these gentlemen is suffering from the same problem, but for different reasons. Years ago, their stories would have remained silent, but today, society has become a bit more relaxed when talking about male libido. For that reason, men are becoming more open to asking for help. I have every reason to believe that Ross and Jake both will be able to overcome their performance anxiety symptoms and once again, return to the sex life they previously enjoyed.

DEPRESSION

There have been many studies on what causes erectile dysfunction. The results vary from one to another, largely in part because the same people are not in each study. One commonality among those studies, though, is that the men who report to have ED often claim to be depressed or have symptoms of depressions. In one study, that percentage was more than 80 percent. Also labeled as a condition or illness, depression is a strong emotion which can impact desire. However, it should be noted that it is difficult to determine in each case if the depression came first and contributed to ED, or if ED was the factor which triggered depression.

ALCOHOL

While alcohol might not necessarily decrease desire, it can significantly impair function, not only when walking, talking, or driving. The beverage that makes you let your hair down can also let an erection down. A drink or two can result in released inhibitions, but consuming larger quantities can result in impotence. Why? Alcohol is a depressant which negatively impacts the central nervous system, resulting in a loss of sensation or inability to register stimulation. It also can cause ED by restricting blood flow to the penis. The remedy? Limit your alcohol intake if you plan on having sexual intercourse.

TOBACCO

Cigarette smoke contains 4,000 different chemicals. The average cigarette contains hundreds of ingredients, of which as many as 50 are carcinogens, or cancer-causing agents. Is it any wonder doctors advise their patients to stop smoking? Tobacco use can result in many health problems, including heart attacks, cancer, and emphysema, but did you know that tobacco can also cause erectile dysfunction? It negatively impacts the heart, blood vessels, and hormones and can result in the loss of blood flow to the penis. Like alcohol, small doses of tobacco are considered to be a stimulant, but larger doses, especially over long periods of time, turn tobacco into a depressant, which again can interfere with the nerve signals that can impair the ability to get an erection. So if you smoke, you have one more benefit to add to the reasons why you should quit.

RECREATIONAL DRUGS

Since smoking and drinking alcohol can impact a man's ability to get or maintain an erection, it should come as no surprise that recreational or illegal drugs can, too. Marijuana has been part of this controversy for years because many claim that it is a safe drug. However, a recent study was performed by Dr. Rany Shamloul, a postdoctoral fellow in the Department of Pharmacology and Toxicology at Queen's University. The research conducted reveals that there is a likely correlation between the use of cannabis and a man's ability to perform. Several of his studies have shown that marijuana affects the abilities of animals to perform. How? Research tells us that cannabis affects brain receptors, and of particular interest, those receptors that deal with sexual functions. Recent research also suggests that those receptors can also be found in the penis, and when they are affected by cannabis, the male may be more likely to suffer from ED.

Marijuana isn't the only drug, though, that impairs sexual function. Cocaine is commonly named as the cause of temporary impotence, and after extended years of usage, can cause permanent damage to the nerves which impact erections. Barbiturates, methadone, and heroin are also among the illegal drugs that can impair sexual function. These drugs can each impact a man's erection differently, but it should be noted that prolonged use of any of them can result in damage to the blood vessels and permanent erectile dysfunction. Over time, illegal and recreational drugs can cause serious damage to your blood vessels, and hence result in permanent erectile dysfunction.

PHYSICAL CAUSES OF ED

While I do see cases of performance anxiety daily, it's also true that many of our patients can attribute their erectile dysfunction to medical problems. In fact, as I pointed out earlier, the majority of our patients have a medical problem that has affected their ability to become erect or ejaculate. Too often, they aren't aware that they have a medical problem or they don't know that their particular health issue is the contributing factor to their performance problem. I sincerely believe if more men were aware that their problem is related to a medical problem, that they wouldn't be so reluctant to seek treatment for their condition.

The fact of the matter is often diseases themselves cause erectile dysfunction. Sometimes, the medication or treatment for the disease is the culprit, and sometimes still it's a combination of the two. Let's take a look at the most common medical conditions and diseases that affect the male erection.

Diabetes: Diabetes causes a lack of blood flow to the nerves in the body. The lack of blood flow is the reason why diabetics have problems with the circulation in their legs and feet. The loss of nerve sensation that results is the reason they're advised to prevent injury to prone areas. Simply put, in more extreme cases, if a diabetic is injured, he may not be able to feel the pain, which is a signal to the body that something is wrong. It's that loss of sensation that causes erectile dysfunction in diabetic males. While injury usually isn't an issue, the loss of sensation and lack of blood flow certainly are. After all, it's increased blood flow that causes an erection, and the ability to be stimulated is also important in both achieving and maintaining an erection.

Erectile dysfunction in diabetic males is not uncommon. In fact, a large number of men with diabetes experience ED. Unfortunately, diabetes doubles the risk.

With treatment, though, even patients with reduced blood flow can resume a normal sex life. It's also true that people with little or no feeling in the penis can achieve and maintain an erection.

One patient came to our clinic seeking help. He was a diabetic, and sadly, he had lost all penile feeling. With the inability to feel, one might wonder why he wanted to be able to resume an active sex life. His story is an interesting one, and one that I found to be unselfish and touching. As he explained his situation, he revealed that he wasn't seeking treatment for himself—he was there for his wife. Although he couldn't feel the pleasure produced by sex, he didn't want to deprive her of that pleasure. He knew that it wasn't possible to recapture his lost sensation, but he was hoping that a treatment was available that would allow him to recapture the ability to please his wife. I found his story and justification for seeking treatment most admirable. It came as a reminder that love is a powerful incentive—people sincerely want to please the people they love. It also came as a stark reminder that sex plays a very important role in sustaining relationships. This gentleman humbly admitted the fear that if he couldn't satisfy his wife, she might leave him or have an affair. I was more than happy to help him regain his ability to make love to his wife and erase that fear.

Kidney Disease is another disease that affects penile health. There are several reasons: First, like diabetes, it affects circulation and nerve function. Kidney disease also impacts hormone production and energy levels, both of which also affect a healthy and active sex life. Due to those changes, as well as the fact that kidney disease has been known to reduce a man's sex drive, it's common that men who suffer from kidney disease also have some level of ED. These symptoms are also exacerbated by the fact that many of the preferred drugs prescribed for kidney disease have the same side effects as the disease itself. If the disease isn't the problem, the medicine is. With both of these risk factors at play, it's not surprising that half of the men suffering from kidney failure also suffer from erectile dysfunction.

Neurological diseases: Neurological diseases are diseases of the nerves and/or brain. Because an erection relies on signals from the brain to stimulate the nerves in the penis, men with these diseases are at high risk for ED. Examples of common neurological diseases are strokes, Parkinson's disease, multiple sclerosis, Alzheimer's, and injuries to the spinal cord or brain.

Vascular disease: Vascular is a medical term that relates to blood vessels, arteries, and the circulatory system. Again, this is yet another disease that limits the flow of blood to the penis. ED patients who suffer from vascular disease are often diagnosed with hypertension (high blood pressure), high levels of cholesterol, or hardening of the arteries, a condition known as atherosclerosis. Some of these patients have had a heart attack at some point in their past. Diseases in this category constitute one of the major physical causes of erectile dysfunction. It's also true that the drugs which are used to treat vascular diseases also have side effects that affect a man's sex drive.

A perfect example is the case of Pat, a male who had just turned 30. He was married and the father of two daughters. He and his wife had an active sex life until a required annual physical exam for work revealed that he had high blood pressure. Because Pat's family had a history of high blood pressure and heart disease, he was immediately placed on medication to return his blood pressure to acceptable levels. His blood pressure dropped, but so did his sex drive—to the point that it was non-existent. After a couple months, Pat did some research and found out that many medications prescribed for his condition affect a man's libido. With over 200 different medications to choose from, his doctor was able to prescribe a different one and return his sex life to its previous active state.

Prostate surgery: Prostate surgery is often the treatment for prostate cancer. Prostate cancer isn't known to cause erectile dysfunction, but the treatment for the prostate cancer, including surgery, radiation and hormone therapy, is a common cause of ED. Prostate surgery affects a man's sexual health because it can damage or require the removal of tissues and nerves in the genital area, resulting in an ability to achieve or maintain erection.

My foster father had prostate cancer, and it is becoming more frequently diagnosed. Whether that's because there is an increase in the number of men who have prostate cancer, or if it's simply the result of more frequent and earlier screenings, along with the increase, we've seen an increase in the number of men who seek treatment for ED.

Hormones: It's true that testosterone plays a role in a sexual stimulation. When there is an imbalance, or a reduction, of testosterone and other hormones, such as thyroid hormones, a man's sex drive can be impacted.

While that list of psychological and physical causes of erectile dysfunction isn't all encompassing, it's a good representation of some of the most common causes of ED.

As you can see, our overall health plays a very active and important role in our sexual health. It's also true that our brain has a significant role. Contrary to popular misconception, erections don't start in the penis. They start in the brain, and then can only be achieved if there are no interruptions in blood flow or in the transmission of signals to the nerves of the penis. I believe that if more people understood the huge impact that the brain and our health have on a man's ability to achieve an erection, men would be more likely to seek treatment and we'd be able to remove the embarrassment when discussing sexual health. It's true that erectile dysfunction is the name given to a condition, but it's also true that ED is a symptom, not a disease. And as in many other medical symptoms or problems, there is a treatment that is available.

Chapter Three

PREMATURE EJACULATION

"IF YOU DON'T FIX ME, I'm going to kill myself." Those words came from a handsome college athlete. He had just broken up with a beautiful girl, and the defining factor in the end of their relationship was that this young, healthy man's sexual ability lasted no more than a few mere seconds. After suffering several embarrassing attempts, he finally gave up, resigning himself to the fact that his fate was sealed. Like so many of our patients have expressed, he thought, *Oh well, what's the use? I'll probably finish too soon.* It truly is self-sabotaging. Premature ejaculation and performance anxiety are very real and they're very damaging to a man's confidence and self-esteem.

But yet, like the college athlete, most men who suffer from premature ejaculation and performance anxiety suffer in silence. They think that something must be terribly wrong with their masculinity. They're ashamed, and those emotions spill over into their relationships.

To give you an idea how devastating the effects are, I'd like to share the story of another patient. At the end of an interview with this man, he stopped me as I reached for the door handle and said, "I'll be honest, Dr. Hornsby, I haven't had sex with my wife for 20 years—it's just too humiliating."

Twenty years! Twenty long years of protecting himself from humiliation. Twenty years of depriving himself and his wife of one of the most natural and intimate aspects of a loving relationship. At that moment in time, there was nobody I wanted to help more. I was determined to do everything in my power to make sure that this man could go home, grab his wife, and make up for 20 years of sexless marriage. To my relief, I was able to help him. I could just see the weight that he had been carrying around for two decades fall off his shoulders. I don't know who was more elated—him or me, but I happen to suspect that his reasons surpassed mine by far.

The feelings conveyed by these two men are indicative of many men with premature ejaculation (or PE). It's also not as uncommon as one might think. In fact, more than one-third of all males suffer from PE at some point in their lives. For some, it's occasional and temporary; for others, it's a chronic condition that makes them retreat from sex altogether—it's simply too embarrassing and humiliating.

Premature ejaculation is defined as ejaculation which occurs with little sexual stimulation, usually before the man prefers it to happen. For some men, this happens before intercourse occurs, while others may experience it within seconds of penetration.

Premature ejaculation often stems from oversensitivity and nervousness. It's a vicious cycle—one episode of PE can inject so much anxiety in a man that his fear of repeating this inability to perform to his satisfaction compounds the situation, making it much worse. The end result? A man whose self-esteem plummets as he lives in internal fear of embarrassment. Eventually, he deprives himself of the potential for any sexual pleasure, thinking that the risk is far greater than any reward.

In reality, it's self-defeating. The fear of premature ejaculation only serves to contribute to its occurrence. A man ultimately finds himself pacing nervously outside the bedroom door, trying to talk himself into giving it one last try while simultaneously talking himself out of it. One of the factors at play here is negative feedback as a man evaluates his own sexual performance.

That self-evaluation begins relatively early in a man's life. A man's sexuality begins when he's young. By the time he is a teenager, he's exploring that sexuality. His hormones are awakening and becoming very active. As a result, so is his curiosity and his desire. He knows from health class and the birds and bees talk that if he has sex, he can now father a child. Because of his young age, lack of experience, and his fear of fathering a child, it's likely that he'll explore his sexuality alone through masturbation.

Realizing that this is a sensitive issue for a teenager, and yes, many adults, the boy is likely to fear being caught in the act of masturbating. So, to prevent such embarrassment, he'll take precautions, such as locking doors and hurrying the process. That's very understandable...but he teaches himself something when he does that. Unconsciously, in his mind, sex, and in particular ejaculation, becomes hurried. Learning to undo these ingrained thoughts and behaviors can be difficult, and they can also be one reason why a man has problems with premature ejaculation in the future.

The treatment of premature ejaculation is a complex process. Thankfully, modern medicine has evolved in this area. No longer are physicians limited to yesterday's past ineffective treatments, such as anti-depressants, positive feedback, and bio-therapy. The results of those treatments were proven too often to be inadequate. For doctors, the focus of treatment usually relied on one area—the brain or the body. But now, we know that the most effective way to treat PE is to disconnect the body from the mind.

How does it work? As I vividly remember explaining to a 28-year-old patient who announced that if I couldn't fix his problem, he couldn't keep living, we need to approach PE from a different angle. Because erections and ejaculation are both triggered in the mind by stimuli, we need to offer a treatment that allows the erection to continue, even after that stimuli has been received.

Simply put, forget about anti-depressants. Depression isn't the underlying cause of premature ejaculation—it's a symptom of it. Today, I treat PE with a more effective method. By providing a patient with medication that enables him to have an erection that is totally disconnected from his thought processes, he can give both himself and his partner satisfaction and enjoyment while building his self-esteem.

It's rather innovative, but one of the most common-sense solutions available. The first time a man takes the medication and has sex, he will ejaculate as he always does—early. But as soon as he climaxes, he'll realize that he is still erect. Now, he has a second chance to satisfy his partner. This time, however, ejaculation will be delayed because it's so soon after the first time. With each ability to delay orgasm, his self-esteem gets real positive feedback and he lasts longer. The cycle then continues, this time in a positive, not self-defeating, manner.

The men I've treated for PE range in age. Some are in their upper teens, while others are in their mid-50s. Most of them have tried the age-old psychological techniques to overcome PE, and many have resorted to drugs, prescribed or otherwise. I've even heard of some men taking the street drug ecstasy, hoping it would help. I caution all of my patients not to endanger themselves by taking any drug that is illegal. The risk is far too great, the effectiveness is far too uncertain, and there are proven ways to combat premature ejaculation.

I'd also like to point out that erectile dysfunction and premature ejaculation go hand in hand. It's not uncommon for a patient who experiences one of these conditions to experience both. The correlation occurs often enough that when I treat a patient for ED, the same treatment is also used for PE.

Effectively treating premature ejaculation is one of the most rewarding things I do in my specialty. In the past, the solutions have been few and far between, ranging from psychological exercises that train a man to change his thoughts from sex to another subject, like cleaning the garage, to physical exercises which strengthen the muscles, supposedly allowing a man to "stop" his ejaculation before it occurs. Those methods have fallen short and provided little, if any, relief to most men. And, as you can see, each of those methods focuses on only one area—the body or the mind. By providing a treatment that takes into account the mind and the body, we've finally found an effective way to lessen the physical symptoms of premature ejaculation, while simultaneously addressing prevention by reinforcing the mind.

Chapter Four

INJURY AND ILLNESS

SOME MIGHT THINK THAT SEXUAL activity would be the last thing on a man's mind if he's injured or diagnosed with an illness. On the contrary, I've found that it's often times when the good health we take for granted comes into question that men seek closeness and intimacy with their partner. Unfortunately, at a time when there is an increased desire to strengthen the bond that comes from sexual relations with the person we love, the health issue or the treatment of it interferes with the ability to do so.

Indeed, a satisfactory sex life produces more than feelings of temporary pleasure—for both men and women, especially during trying times, it's validation of life and love. Reaching for the person we love is a natural response that conveys our need for support and comfort. In an online forum, one gentleman anonymously related how illness impacted his sex life and his marriage:

I started having trouble to "get it up" during sex because of prostate cancer radiation treatments. It was very frustrating and it bothered me a lot. Although, my wife assured me she still loved me no matter what. But I could feel our sexual relationship was not the same and that put a strain on our marriage.

The increase in prostate cancer diagnoses translates to more men who have a decreased ability to perform. Due to its location in the body, the prostate has an impact on a man's sexual organs. In fact, erectile dysfunction is one symptom of both benign and malignant prostate diseases.

The side effect of his treatment caused the man in our example to suffer from erectile dysfunction, a common symptom of radiation, chemotherapy, or surgery. It's one reason why some men put off prostate cancer screening.

Yes, there are other reasons, including the discomfort of the exam. I believe more men would willingly abide by the screening guidelines if they knew that it's also possible to detect prostate cancer through blood tests.

Let's step back a minute and review the guidelines for prostate cancer, then we'll move forward and talk about the treatment options and how they affect a man's sexual health.

New guidelines recommend that prostate screening begin at the age of 50. However, African Americans and those with a high risk or family history of prostate cancer should begin screening five years earlier, at the age of 45.

This discussion is more relevant today than it was in the past. Prostate cancer has gained considerable attention, largely because it affects 1 out of every 6 men. The number of cases has been on the upswing, making it more likely that a man will be diagnosed with prostate cancer than a woman will be of receiving a breast cancer diagnosis. African Americans do have a higher risk than Caucasians; other risk factors include age (the older a man is, the more likely he is to have prostate cancer) and family history.

Of those men who are diagnosed with or treated for prostate cancer, many suffer from erectile dysfunction. In fact, one-third to one-half of the men I treat have had prostate surgery or a radical prostatectomy.

One of the reasons that prostate surgery results in ED is that the prostate rests between two groups of nerves— the same nerves that tell the penis to produce an erection. During surgery, those nerves can be removed or damaged. Thankfully, there are less invasive treatments available today than radical prostatectomy. However, even in the most delicate surgery, utilizing the finest techniques carried out by the best of surgeons, there is a risk of injuring those nerves.

The nerves that surround the prostate are indeed very fine. I liken them to the tiny fiber-like threads in the hair net my grandmother used to wear. Years ago, men had no option but to undergo a radical prostatectomy, but medical innovation has blessed us with less invasive, nerve-sparing surgeries which can limit or prevent damage to these sensitive nerves. Regardless of the procedure performed, however, prostate surgery, like any other surgical procedure, is invasive and can be traumatic on the body.

For example, one of the men who has impacted me the most in my life experienced some major side effects of prostate surgery. His surgery occurred more than ten years ago, not long ago by some standards, but significant in the medical field. At that time, treatment options were very limited. Beyond the time of his surgery, he experienced a great deal of difficulty with his sexuality. He suffered from urinary incontinence and a greatly reduced ability to maintain an erection. While I certainly wish that less invasive options were available to him at the time of his surgery, I'm glad to say that the side effects he experienced from surgery were treatable.

Prostate cancer is treatable, but so are the sexual side effects. If more men knew that, I do believe they wouldn't be so reluctant to undergo annual screenings and seek treatment for what can be a highly treatable disease. The quality of life does not have to diminish when saving life; a man can treat prostate cancer without losing his sexuality or ability to perform.

Other surgeries which impact a man's libido include heart surgery. Traditional open heart surgery, after all, is very invasive. However, today there are less traumatic options, including robotic surgery and angioplasty. Those who undergo the more radical surgery do require a longer recovery time. Still, both groups might experience some degree of erectile dysfunction.

One of the main reasons for this is psychological. It's true that heart surgery can be life altering. It's a wake-up call that reminds us that our life depends on our heart health. We begin to take better care of ourselves, eat healthier foods, and implement a moderate exercise program. Yet, the fact that a man has had a heart attack or heart surgery can result in fear of having sex. Of course, the advice of your cardiologist or cardiac surgeon should always be sought and followed. But if you are given your doctor's consent to resume sexual activity, there is no reason why you shouldn't.

It's not uncommon, though, for men to experience difficulty achieving or maintaining an erection after experiencing heart problems. Sure, the desire is there, but as soon as an erection begins to occur, the little voice in their head stops it, reminding them to be scared that having sex will trigger a heart attack. This isn't likely. More than 80% of men who have had a heart attack can resume sexual activity without any problems. For some, though, the increased heart rate that occurs during sex is misconstrued as heart palpitations.

During sex, the heart rate does increase to about 115 beats per minute. This heart rate is likened to the increase one would experience after climbing stairs, a brisk walk, or riding a bike. If you can participate in those activities without any unpleasant sensation or discomfort, you should be able to enjoy sex, as well. Again, it's getting past that mental block that's trying to protect you. The patients I've treated for this have been able to overcome that fear and engage in sexual activity.

I should point out, too, that some medications used to treat heart disease and ailments also impact sexual health. High blood pressure medications can impact a man's libido, as well as reduce the amount of zinc in the body, which is an important ingredient in the production of testosterone. Some beta blockers are also responsible for a decreased sex drive or a loss of circulation, both which affect the ability to achieve an erection or have an orgasm. In that case, hormone replacement therapy can be an effective counter.

I've already discussed the effects of diabetes on a man's sexual health. Regulating blood sugar and following the prescribed treatment of your doctor will help prevent sexual problems stemming from this disease. In the past, the circulatory and nerve problems that are associated with diabetes and result in ED were considered an unfortunate, but unavoidable, side effect. Today, though, we know that diabetes does not have to be the kiss of death to a satisfying sex life. I have many former patients who are a testament to that fact.

Along with illnesses, injuries can also affect a man's sex drive or sexual ability. Spinal-cord injuries are one, and I'm glad that there has been increased attention on helping men regain sexual function after such an injury. Other types of injuries which affect a man's sexual performance are brain injuries, penile injuries, body-disfiguring injuries, and injuries which interfere with nerves or blood flow. With treatment for the emotional or physical problems these injuries cause, I've witnessed many victims of accidents or injury regain their sexual desire and ability.

Chapter Five

MEN'S ANDROPAUSE

MEN IN THEIR EARLY 40'S experience a decline in a cluster of hormones called Andropause. This is similar to the menopause females experience. I'm not referring to hot flashes, but rather a time in a man's life when he begins to notice subtle changes, like a decrease in penis size, semen volume, muscle mass, and energy levels. At the same time that he sees reductions in those areas, he could also notice an increase in other symptoms, like insomnia and irritability. Physically and emotionally, all of these factors affect a man's ability to maintain a healthy sex life.

There has long been controversy over whether men do, indeed, experience this "menopause-like" condition. For years, many have believed that it manifests in the form of a mid-life crisis. That mid-life crisis indicates a life change brought about by the aging process. It could stem from anything, but most people will agree that it is a man's attempt to recapture his lost youth. While the process is actual and from real body chemistry changes, it affects a whole spectrum of symptoms from psychological to sexual in range.

Clinically speaking, this male menopause is recognized, and it has a name—Andropause. The symptoms of Andropause include much more than an urge to buy a red Corvette and prove our masculinity by attracting the attention of young ladies 20 years our junior. It's the result of a reduction of testosterone, which many experience between the ages of 45 and 60.

Known as the sex hormones, this cluster of chemicals is responsible for more than a man's sexual urges—they produce the larger bone and muscle mass in adult men. Present in male infants in the womb, it's these sex-related hormones that stimulate the sexual development that differentiate between boys and girls.

The effects of a drop in andropausal hormone levels are felt to some degree by many males. Physically, the resulting reduction in bone mass can lead to fractures, as well as a higher percentage of impotence among men in this age bracket. This impotence can reveal itself in the form of erectile dysfunction or in a noticeable drop in a man's sex drive. What was once an important part of a man's life wanes and becomes less significant to him.

Psychologically, though, these sex hormones are necessary for the male psyche. Men do define themselves by their sexual performance—it's part of who we are in both body and mind. So, when andropausal hormone levels fall, it's not surprising that the male psyche and self-worth also decline. In short, he sees himself as less of a man and suffers a loss of pride. This is where the mid-life crisis comes in—making a man want to go out and prove his masculinity as he attempts to chase and reclaim his pride.

A male's sex hormone levels are highest in his 20's, which makes sense because that's also a time when his sexual desire is at its highest. Low levels are more commonly seen in mid-life; however, many young men have been diagnosed with premature Andropause. At puberty, these hormones deepen the voice and produce facial, chest, and pubic hair. It is responsible for a young teen's obsession with sex. Young or old, low andropause symptoms on a long-term basis can result in major physical problems, including an increased risk of heart attack, strokes, prostate cancer, dementia, and hip fractures.

For those reasons, we should not view Andropause solely from a sexual perspective. The physical and mental manifestations are serious and should never be ignored. Society, though, and its silence of anything to do with a man's sexual organs or performance have led many to sweep this issue under the rug, where it can't be seen. Too often, the stigma that shrouds male sexuality is the reason men accept these unwanted changes in their body, attributing their lack of energy and lower sex drive to problems at the office or simply growing old.

Decreasing andropausal hormone levels can be at play in cases of ED or weakening erections. The trend can also be reversed. Through secondary andropausal therapy, we can slowly reverse the symptoms, thus helping men regain their libido, strength, and energy, while reducing the irritability and grumpiness that also accompanies a reduction in testosterone.

In the past, abuse by athletes handed hormone replacement therapy a bad name. I'd like to reverse that once and for all. When used properly, it can do so much more than boost a man's psyche and make him a superstar pitcher—it can make a difference in every aspect of a man's life—from improving his relationships and self-esteem to reducing the risk of life-threatening diseases and loss of memory. That's why I often include andropausal support therapy in the treatment of my patients. Andropause has implications which stretch far and wide.

SEEKING TREATMENT

Chapter Six

REACHING OUT

AS A PHYSICIAN SPECIALIZING IN male sexual health, I take a heightened notice of the public and professional reluctance to openly discuss the issues which revolve around my field. Every time I see a magazine display, there are multiple front cover headlines advertising articles which relate to female sexual and reproductive health. From articles relating new sex positions to enhance arousement or achieve orgasm, ways to conquer tired-mom syndrome and increase sexual desire, and how to recognize signs of endometriosis or ovarian cysts, women's magazines have it covered. The fact of the matter is that females are not as reluctant or shy as men to openly discuss their sexual health. The media has enabled such openness by making women's sexual health an "accepted" and newsworthy topic of discussion. It's very common to see newspaper articles, reporting medical facts, treatments, or stories about women overcoming infertility or ovarian cancer. The same is not true for men's sexual health, and the double standard is one that I address every day. How often do you pick up the newspaper or a national magazine and read a feature article about a man who has suffered from or overcome erectile dysfunction?

I've long been an advocate of bringing male sexual health to the attention of the public. The time to take it out of the bedroom and from behind closed doors is long past due. Reluctance to do so has prevented many a man from seeking treatment for conditions which are very treatable. The stigma surrounding male sex organs must be erased to open that door of discussion so men will be more comfortable admitting they have a problem and seeking help for it.

Does a man's shame or humiliation stem from the fact that unlike a woman, his sexual organs can be seen? Unlike the rest of the anatomy, the penis is not hidden. However, since childhood, we've been cautioned that it's a "private" part that shouldn't be seen or talked about. We carry that admonition with us into adulthood, unfortunately, allowing it to cloud more than acceptable topics of conversation as we let it impede the ability to enjoy a very natural function—and one which I might add is the reason our body is designed the way it is. Sure, sex can stay behind closed doors, but sexual health doesn't have to—it should come as no secret that our bodies are specifically designed not only for sex, but also to reap pleasure during intimate relations.

There are statistics which reveal the number of males who suffer from a loss of libido, erectile dysfunction, or premature ejaculation, but because of the code of silence adopted by many men, one must wonder about their accuracy. That same code of silence is the one that interferes with our ability to reach these men and share effective, new treatments that can bring them relief. It is, indeed, a catch-22—they won't know what we can do to help them unless they contact us—and we can't reach them until they do.

Shame and embarrassment are powerful emotions. Sadly, they're also commonly attributed to erectile dysfunction or premature ejaculation. I'd like to set the record straight, though. The inability to perform is a medical problem, not an indication of a man's masculinity or manhood. Let's reserve shame and embarrassment for things we can control, like lying to your spouse about money or showing disrespect to your mother. Be humiliated when you knowingly do something wrong if you wish, but don't be humiliated because your body is not functioning the way it should.

When we remove the personal negative connotations behind male sexuality, we will finally be able to treat the men who suffer so much because of it. In the last decade, the little blue pill, Viagra®, has helped increase awareness to a degree, but it's not enough. For one thing, Viagra® and similar medications, don't work for every man, leaving him to believe that something must *really* be wrong with him (and thus creating an even greater loss of self-esteem). In addition, because these medications have become recreational for some who use them to increase the length of time their healthy erection lasts, those who have real problems achieving or maintaining an erection are even less inclined to admit they have a problem.

There is a real need for disclosure in my specialty. In order for me to help these men, they must open the door and the discussion. But because of the stigma that surrounds the male body and sexual performance, when they do open the door, I must ensure extreme privacy. Women don't face such obstacles. When she visits the gynecologist, she doesn't fear embarrassment that a neighbor or coworker will see her. For men, though, the opposite holds very true.

That embarrassment occurs before the first office visit, usually starting with the initial phone call to make an appointment. Men who call are afraid to ask questions, reluctant to provide their name, and fearful that their privacy will be violated and they'll become the laughingstock of the guys at the gym. It doesn't have to be that way.

In all of my clinics, privacy is a top priority. That's precisely why our offices are not included in a medical complex. Our offices are located in business, not medical, complexes, and our name is not on the door or posted on a sign. Men who visit our office take comfort in the fact that from all appearances, they could easily be visiting their accountant or business consultant.

I know that it's a sensitive issue and most men don't want to bump into their neighbor or mother-in-law when they're walking out the door. In all interactions, from the way we address and communicate with our male patients, to the billing process, we exercise discretion. It's just one way we try to overcome the embarrassment and sensitivity common among our patients.

The respect for privacy is one thing the medical profession should exercise if they truly want to offer men viable treatments that can provide them with physical and emotional relief. I believe a man should feel as comfortable and at ease picking up the phone to make an appointment for a consultation with a sexual health specialist as he is when ordering a pizza. Okay, maybe not that comfortable, but in my opinion, there is no reason why he should be any less comfortable than when making an appointment for any other medical issue.

To make it easier for our patients, we operate with an all-male staff. While there certainly are many excellent female doctors, nurses, and support personnel, we opt to employ highly-qualified male personnel because we know that it's difficult for men to discuss sexual problems with women, especially women they don't already know. Any man who calls our clinic can rest assured that he will be greeted and assisted by a competent *male* professional whose job relies upon exercising total discretion.

Discretion is a key factor in why I chose to focus my career and practice solely on men's sexual health. It's true that I could treat ED and PE while practicing other forms of medicine. I could have an appointment book that includes visits for migraines and hypertension, as well as a smattering of men with performance issues. But, that's all I'd treat—a smattering, a pebble's ripple in the large pool of men who can benefit from treatment. By focusing on this one area, I can assure my patients that they won't feel as self-conscious as they would intermingled in a waiting room with patients who have other medical problems. In fact, it should put their mind at ease that they don't stand out in the crowd—here, they are among the norm.

In order to reach out to our patients, and in order for them to feel comfortable reaching out to us, it's critical that every step of the process takes into consideration the male psyche and his desire for privacy. In short, the physician and/or the clinic must continually exercise discretion and view every communication and contact from the patient's point of view. That is a level of respect that every patient deserves, and a standard we must all adhere to. Once a patient walks through our door, they'll notice a difference from other medical offices. We don't announce their name to a waiting room full of people, and we don't plaster our name on our door, invoices, or correspondence. If requested, we'll use only frat names to make men feel more comfortable. These are small measures that we hope will put a man's mind at ease, knowing that his privacy is safe when he walks through our door. We need to have an inviting welcome mat, but one that's on the inside of the door—not the outside.

Chapter Seven

PERSONAL AND FAMILY HISTORY

WHAT DOES YOUR FAMILY HISTORY have to do with your sex life? Maybe nothing. Maybe everything. It depends on what the problem is, what's causing it, and your genetics.

A patient might walk into my office and want to get to the core of his problem—*now*. In a hurry to get in and get out, some want to tell me what's wrong and get a one-size-fits-all cure so they can quickly and inconspicuously leave. But it's not always that easy.

Our clinic, like any other, will ask personal questions, and we'll want a comprehensive medical history—yours, as well as others in your family. One reason is because we believe in curing the cause of your problem, not just treating the symptom. Therefore, it's important for us to know what other medical issues you might be experiencing or have experienced in the past.

I realize that it's likely that you won't know if your father experienced ED, and I don't expect that you would know. However, if you have a family history of prostate enlargement or cancer, sharing that information could do more than help your sexual issues; it can be the piece of information that can help to prevent or treat a medical problem. The same holds true for heart or vascular disease, diabetes, or bladder or kidney problems. All genetic diseases are important for any physician to know.

Because many patients come to us for performance problems, we must be cautious that we don't neglect the possibility of a medical problem. After all, medical problems are the most common cause of performance difficulties. It comes as a surprise to some men to find that their recent ED instances stem from a medical problem they don't even know about. That's one more reason why I encourage men to seek treatment for ED and PE—often, we can uncover a potential health problem or risk that has the potential to become serious without intervention.

So, when your doctor asks questions that don't pertain specifically to you, it's not because they're poking around into your personal life just to be nosy. There's a reason we ask for a full medical history and also a reason why we ask personal questions, wanting to know when you last had sex without a problem, how often you have or used to have sex, and even what's going on in your personal relationships and at work. Experience has proven time and again that all of these factors play a major role in a man's ability to perform— even if he doesn't know it.

Are you doing yourself a favor by failing to disclose information? Usually, the answer is no. Could you actually be delaying finding the solution to your problems? That's a strong possibility. By not sharing certain details or downplaying others, you could be keeping a key piece of information that is the one piece of the puzzle that helps us find the source of your problem and the treatment that works best for you.

That's one area where personalities play a role. First, we know that a sense of trust with medical personnel is necessary before you're comfortable sharing intimate details. You need to be assured of confidentiality, while feeling a genuine and sincere concern for your situation and health. For that reason, your doctor may feel like he needs to 'break the ice,' which helps the patient-doctor relationship cross the stranger threshold. That's one reason I like my patients to know my background and strive to let them know that I'm no different than them. I do understand that my specialty requires me to be approachable.

One of my patients expressed surprise when I was the physician that walked in the room. He had read about our clinic in a *Physician Times Today* magazine that featured my picture on the cover. Because of the publicity, he mistakenly thought I had too much prestige to actually be seeing patients. He honestly expected to be seen by a different doctor, and he told me so. After introducing myself and explaining to him that successfully treating patients is the most rewarding part of my career, he changed his perception. Rather than being in awe, he was able to forget about me and focus on his problems.

Getting past any misconceptions or discomfort is one of our priorities. Because patients don't often know what medical or family issues may be impacting them, a conversation needs to take place to help pull that information forward. Expect to be asked questions like:

- Have you or any member of your family had diabetes or been diagnosed with an enlarged prostate?
- Have any members of your immediate family had a heart attack or been diagnosed with high blood pressure or heart disease?
- Has your father, grandfather, or brother had

prostate surgery?

- Do you wake up often during the night with a need to urinate (a symptom of an enlarged prostate)?
- Are you on any medications? (Be prepared to provide a full accounting of prescribed, over-the-counter, and other medications or drugs you are taking.)
- Have you or a member of your immediate family been diagnosed with kidney, bladder, colon, or vascular disease?
- Have you suffered an injury to the brain or spinal cord?
- Do you have any known allergies? What are they?
- And, of course, the typical, "Do you drink, smoke, or use recreational drugs?"

Along with your medical and family history, a doctor will want a full accounting of your sex life. When did you notice a problem? Has it been ongoing and continual? Does it come and go? How frequently? Did it occur suddenly or gradually? What, if anything, has changed in your life around the time that you noticed a problem? What, if anything, have you already tried (Viagra®, Cialis®, herbal supplements, etc.)? Have you ever consulted with a physician for your problem? Have you previously received a diagnosis, or are you currently under a physician's care for any problem, including sexual or performance problems?

You might recognize many of these questions as the same ones you're asked when you see your family doctor for something like bronchitis or an ear infection. That's because they are. The reason I'd ask the same questions brings us back to the reality that erectile dysfunction is usually the result of a medical problem. Treating it is medicine. We prescribe only drugs that meet FDA approval, and all of our prescriptions are filled by a licensed pharmacist. Again, it's justification that the body's sexual organs are not separate from any other body function or purpose. A man's anatomy is part of, not separate, from his body. Everything works together, and if one part doesn't function properly, the rest is likely to be impacted to some degree.

As you can see, the first visit to our office is a fact-finding venture. The answers are all pieces of a puzzle that help your physician find the treatment that will be most effective for you, considering your medical, family, and personal history. The difference between our clinic and other doctor offices, though, is that when your first visit is over, you'll already know that you have been prescribed a treatment that works, even when others haven't in the past.

Chapter Eight

POPULAR MEDICATIONS

MANY OF THE PATIENTS WHO come to our clinic have already tried other drugs. They've seen the countless commercials for the three most commonly prescribed ED drugs, Viagra®, Cialis®, and Levitra®. Some of them have had success, at least temporarily, when using those drugs. But unfortunately, 70 percent of the men who have tried them either don't get the results they want or find that, over time, those drugs lose their effectiveness. Still others cannot take them because of the adverse side effects they cause. Let's take a look at those drugs and how they affect men.

VIAGRA®

If there is one thing we can thank the makers of the little blue pill Viagra® for, it's the role its marketing efforts have played in letting men know that there are treatments for ED. In fact, the introduction of Viagra® (sildenafil citrate) on the national scene created a big sensation among men who were desperately seeking an easy solution to their performance problems. But it also caused quite a stir among men who didn't have any performance problems at all, but who were simply interested in using the drug to enhance their erection, causing it to be firmer or last longer.

Whatever the purpose of taking Viagra®, as a doctor, it's my duty to point out that these drugs, like most, do have side effects—some of which are serious or even life threatening. Here is an overview of some of the more common side effects:

Diarrhea; dizziness; flushing; headache; heartburn; stuffy nose; upset stomach.

Possible severe reactions which warrant immediate medical attention include:

Allergic reactions, such as a rash, itching, swelling (particularly in the mouth or face), and tightness in the chest. Other severe reactions are a prolonged or painful erection; chest pain; fast or irregular heartbeat; dizziness and fainting spells; loss of memory; numbness; one-sided weakness; ringing in the ears; seizure; stroke; cardiac arrest; changes in or loss of vision or hearing.

The truth is that 20 million men have taken Viagra®, but only a small percentage stop taking it because of unwanted side effects. It's more likely that a man would stop taking Viagra® because as his body changes over time, so does the effectiveness of the drug. Simply stated, it doesn't work as well as it once did. But there is still some danger in taking this drug, whether it's prescribed or obtained illegally through a black market non-prescription website or entity (which by the way, is very dangerous—no one knows precisely what goes into those drugs). Here are some comments made by people who have had negative experiences from taking Viagra®:

- *After taking Viagra®, I woke up the next morning with major hearing loss in the left ear. Now have recovered most of hearing, but have constant and unrelenting ringing - actually it's a buzzing - in both ears.*

- *My husband died at the age of 46 from a massive heart attack as a result of taking Viagra®.*

And virtually the same comment by another widow:

- *My husband died at the age of 44 from a massive heart attack caused by the use of Viagra®.*

And here is a sampling of adverse side effects among other users:

- *I have been diagnosed with NAION and lost partial vision in my right eye. The Dr. advised me to stop using Viagra® and Cialis®.*

- *My husband was prescribed Viagra® and he took it, we had relations and then he suffered a heart attack. Is it worth your life?*

- *My husband took lowest dosage of Viagra®/ Cialis®/Levitra® (not sure which was the cause) as post-operative therapy after prostate cancer at age 50. Woke up with severe loss of hearing in one ear three years ago and it has never changed.*

- *Took Viagra® by Dr. and now am blind in my left eye, with no hope for recovery.*

- *Was prescribed Viagra® by Dr. - have taken 50mg doses once a week for last year- 3 wks ago after taking 50mg dose- left eye not functioning. Mini stroke in eye says ophthalmologist. Had MRI on brain—am wearing a patch and going with just one eye - hoping it will reconnect.*

Of course, these examples are not common and indicative of all or even most of the people who take Viagra®. In fact, the majority of users find that they suffer no side effects, or minor ones, like a headache or flushing of the face. Some have been known to seek medical treatment for an erection that won't go away, which contrary to some opinions, is not a good thing. It's painful and a medical emergency.

I believe that there is no such thing as too much information. An informed user of any drug knows the side effects, allergic reactions, and benefits of the drugs their prescriptions. Cedars-Sinai Medical Center in Los Angeles performed an analysis of more than one thousand major medical effects surrounding Viagra®. The majority of them stemmed around cardiovascular problems—some caused death. I don't relate this information as a scare tactic, but as a duty. Yes, major events like these are rare…but they do happen.

It's more common to hear of a man who has sought medical attention from a severely prolonged erection after taking Viagra® or a similar drug. Actually, a prolonged erection is technically one that lasts four hours or more. I should also point out that a prolonged erection is not the same as a painful erection, which is known as priapism, but the two can go hand in hand. While some men may get excited about the prospect of having an erection that lasts for so many hours, when it's an adverse reaction, it can cause penile damage. Ranging from temporary to permanent, the damage to the penis might be the rupture of an artery or a lack of oxygen to the penile tissues. Again, I reiterate that prolonged or painful erections can be a medical emergency and should not be taken lightly.

The big three pharmaceutical drugs used to treat erectile dysfunction also come with a list of restrictions, otherwise known as pre-existing conditions which warrant warnings that men with these conditions should not be prescribed these drugs. Those conditions span a wide variety of ailments, including blood diseases, past strokes or heart conditions, high or low blood pressure, kidney or liver problems, stomach ulcers, and vision loss. This is a good reason to steer clear of ordering Viagra®, Cialis®, or Levitra® online or through a non-prescription market. ED is often a medical problem, and treating it should always be done under the guidance and advice of a physician.

Aside from those who shouldn't take such drugs and those who suffer adverse side effects, are the men who tried them but were disappointed to find that they didn't produce the desired results. One 49-year-old patient expressed his dissatisfaction: "Viagra® helped a little bit, but not as much as I had thought it would. I was disappointed, but I wasn't ready to give up that part of my life."

His story is one I hear every day. It's estimated that as many as 70 percent of the men who suffer from ED don't respond favorably to the most popular drugs. Then there are those who were glad to find that the drugs worked very well, and after some time, found that the effectiveness lessened or stopped altogether. In these instances, the medication didn't change—the man did. Over time, a male's body changes, his testosterone levels fluctuate, and his circulation and nerves might lose some of their effectiveness. For these men, their bodies have outstripped the dosing of medications that once worked.

One man posed a question in an online men's health forum that spoke for many: *Is there anyone else who took Viagra® and it stopped working? Is this normal?* One response indicated that he was not alone, and that a customer service rep of the manufacturer had told him that after some time, it is possible to become immune to the medication.

Viagra®, Cialis®, and Levitra® almost always work initially, which offers a solution, albeit temporary, for some. These drugs fundamentally dilate blood vessels all over the body, including those of the penis, thus producing an erection. Over time, however, the effects of these drugs can, and often do, lessen. It's not because the medications change—it's because a man's body changes. As a man ages, his ability to achieve or maintain an erection might require higher doses of these meds. But that's not always possible; in fact, it's more likely that the patient will find that he's reached the maximum dosage, without receiving the results he once enjoyed from these drugs. As a result, the normal aging process slowly out paces the limited dozing options of these oral medicines. Because the dosage of these medicines can only be adjusted two to three times, men who have been taking them can eventually reach the highest dosage allowed without receiving the desired results.

Once Viagra®, Cialis®, and Levitra® are no longer effective, men find themselves back at square one—this time with seemingly fewer options. Some might find alternate treatment; others give up and begin the process of mourning their sex life. But there are other options, and thankfully, options which allow considerably more dosage adjustments, based on a man's continually changing body and needs. Our medication allows for more than 160 dose adjustments, which allows us to dose and redose based on each man's individual needs. And because our treatment relies on more than one medication, we are able to adjust and readjust prescriptions so they don't become ineffective as a man ages.

When the big three erection drugs fail, some men turn to herbal supplements. Many of the men I treat readily admit that they've fallen prey to ads in the back of magazines and newspapers for herbal preparations. Many of these are not controlled and come from foreign countries—they're not regulated or approved by any health or government agencies; therefore, it's not possible for us to know precisely what ingredients are included in them.

Similar male enhancement supplements can be found in hole-in-the-wall gas stations and convenience stores across the country. Grouped together in displays much like energy boosters and supplements, they claim to be all natural, safe, and effective. Are they? That depends on the product, the individual, and the dosage.

Some of these non-prescription enhancers can affect blood pressure, cause a fast or irregular heartbeat, increase anxiety or bleeding risk, and can also impact the immune system or the body's natural production of hormones. In fact, the FDA has banned some herbal forms of Viagra® due to potent ingredients.

I fully understand why men suffering from impotence would turn to these products. First, they claim to be safe and natural, so they believe that no harm can be done. Second, and probably more important, these products can be purchased over the counter, without a physician's prescription. They're known to be less expensive than their prescription counterparts, and purchasing them in an over-the-counter setting saves the already fragile male psyche from the dreaded embarrassment that can come from seeking medical treatment.

Sadly, there are side effects. Unfortunately, the products don't always work, leaving men with few other well-known options. Many of them have become my patients. Too often, I'm their last resort before their resignation to a sexless life. I feel their pain as they check off the treatments they've already tried that have failed them, and look me in the eye and plead, "Is there anything you can do to help *me*?"

I am confident when I provide them with an answer. "Yes, there is."

Chapter Nine

WHY TREAT ERECTILE DYSFUNCTION AND PREMATURE EJACULATION?

WHAT'S THE BIG DEAL? So a man can't "get it up"—it's not like it'll kill him or something. These are thoughts that run through some people's minds, forming a misconception about the importance of a man's ability to perform. Their basis is as misguided as their opinion. The fact of the matter is, it is a big deal. And it's not just about lust or "getting laid." Maintaining a healthy sex life and the ability to perform impacts so much more...and while the inability to perform may not kill a man, it can pose several hazards to his health.

The truth is that sex is a major part of our overall health and well-being. It's more than having a good time, a romp in the hay, or getting it on. Although the pleasures of sex are, indeed, one of the reasons we seek and enjoy it, sex is not all about fun and play. It's not driven by pure lust, but by our bodies, which are designed to enable our ability to perform, for various reasons.

As a man, I'm aware of the role sex plays in life. As a physician, I'm aware of its contribution toward a man's health. As a husband and father, I've received the rewards it has provided me—a loving and devoted wife and the blessings of fathering beautiful, healthy children. It's a part of every aspect of my life, as it should be for all men.

Because sex has a profound effect on our overall health, it's my hope that every physician would include questions about a patient's sexual desire and ability to perform, at least on an annual basis. The answers can reveal some significant health issues and prevent future problems. Some doctors do this, but others stick to the reason for the visit, walking in the door and asking the patient what their particular health concern is at the time. But by introducing sex-related questions, doctors could gain valuable insight into underlying problems which can cause a domino effect.

A loss of libido, or sexual desire, could indicate a hormonal imbalance. It could also reveal a circulatory problem, a prostate condition, or an emotional problem. When a man loses his sexual desire, suddenly or gradually over time, it's a sign that something is happening, either internally or externally, which is affecting his body's natural ability to perform as it should.

The human body is complex, yet every part of it is designed to work in conjunction with the rest. A male's sexual anatomy is no different than any other part of his body in that respect. Let's quell the popular opinion that a man's penis is separate and apart from the rest of his body—men don't think with their penis—on the contrary, an erection requires the cooperation and participation of the brain, as well as healthy nerve transmission of the signals it emits. The whole process is triggered and stimulated by hormones and carried out through circulation of the blood. Rest assured, the penis isn't an entity all its own—it's an integral part of a man's body, and its health can reveal a lot about a man's health.

Not only does an active sex life depend on good health, it positively contributes to good health. So much so, that the health benefits it produces are a sufficient reason for having sex. Not only does sex feel good, but it's actually good for you. In some cases, it might be just what the doctor ordered. Let's take a look at some of the health benefits sex provides.

Sleep: Sex is conducive to a good night's sleep, as proven by many women's complaint about the uncanny ability a man has to roll over and pass out as soon as he climaxes. But I'd like to set the record straight—he's not doing that because he's insensitive or uncaring—he's simply reacting to the body's natural response to a significant emotional and physical release. This is enhanced by the release of hormones that takes place when orgasm occurs.

A deep restful sleep rejuvenates and recharges the body and the mind. It provides energy to the body and keeps our thought processes sharp. It makes us perform better at work, both physically and emotionally.

Not only is sleep vital to good health, but it's also conducive to good relationships. Tired people are often cranky and irritable, not loving qualities which are appealing and attractive to most. Let's not forget another good reason for sleep—without it, we'd be too tired to have sex. So, sex contributes to a good night's sleep, which in turn contributes to more good sex.

Stress: Sex is one of the biggest stress relievers known to man. As powerful as a workout, it leaves a man feeling calm and relaxed. Why? Well, those same hormones produced by an orgasm which enhance sleep also relieve stress. Oxytocin is the medical name for these hormones, which work to counter the hormones that create stress. When we reduce stress, we're working to prevent many different health issues, including headaches, muscle tension, stomach problems, and high blood pressure.

Reducing stress is also beneficial to our sex life. In fact, relaxation is necessary for a man to achieve an erection. Because an erection is hard, there is misconception that it's tense, like a muscle becomes when flexed. However, the reverse is actually what enables an erection to form—rather than tensing, there must be full relaxation to allow for the entry of the increased blood flow that produces an erection.

Weight Control: Finally, we can acknowledge that there is an exercise that almost everyone enjoys—sex! Sex burns calories, and it gets the heart pumping to a level similar to a moderately strenuous workout. For even greater benefits, increase frequency and duration. So the next time you make a New Year's resolution to lose weight, add a resolution to increase your sexual activity.

Medically, though, it's known that the desire for food and sex are both regulated by the hypothalamus. Add to that the fact that sex also gives the body dopamine, which affects both our appetite for sex and food, and we can see that sex and weight have a direct correlation. At the time of orgasm, dopamine is at its highest. The hormones released when we climax intercept the transmission of dopamine to our brain, thus preventing the brain from getting the signal that the body is craving food.

Of particular benefit is the fact that not only does the act of having sex assist in weight loss or weight control, it's also one of the most powerful incentives for weight loss. We can all attest to the fact that when it comes to sex, we are inspired to look our best and be physically desirable to our partner.

Youthfulness: Sex is the next best thing to the fountain of youth when it comes to countering the effects of age on the body. Orgasms produce DHEA, a steroid hormone that's produced by our adrenal glands, but can also be produced in a man's testes or a woman's ovaries. DHEA precedes the production of sexual hormones, and it reaches its peak in the body during a person's 20's. Around the time a person turns 30, it declines. There have been numerous studies on the connection between a reduction in DHEA and the effects of aging on the body. One study among sexually active 100-year-olds indicates that they had more energy and looked younger than 70-year-olds who were not sexually active. Therefore, by increasing the production of DHEA through sex, one might receive great anti-aging benefits that will make him look younger and live longer.

Pain Relief: Are you sore and achy? Do your joints or muscles hurt? Well, there's a natural pain reliever for what ails you—sex. Yes, those same orgasms that reduce stress and preserve youth also diminish aches and pains. Sex releases powerful endorphins that boost the body's immunity and relieve pain. So the next time you have a headache, rather than reaching for the bottle of Tylenol, try reaching for your partner. It's effective, less expensive, and better for you.

Anti-Depressant: This health benefit is one that I encounter daily in my practice. Virtually every patient I treat for erectile dysfunction or premature ejaculation has expressed some level of depression. Whether this is the result of their condition, other factors in their lives, or both, it's evidence that sex inhibits depression.

Depression makes people sluggish, reducing their productivity. It destroys self-esteem and saps the body and mind from experiencing happiness and pleasure. It's one of the most damaging influences on our overall health and well-being. And often, the side effects of prescription anti-depressant drugs contribute to the problem as they are known to lessen a man's sexual desire and even his ability to climax. In this instance, the cure becomes a part of the problem.

I've witnessed the immediate reversal of depression in men who have had their ability to satisfactorily perform in the bedroom restored. It's partly due to the immediate boost in confidence and self-esteem. It's also attributed to a unique substance in a man's body—semen, which has benefits to both men and women. Semen contains mood enhancers; when men release semen, their mood is elevated. When women receive the semen and it absorbed in the vaginal wall, they, too, are reported to receive the mood-enhancing benefits. This is yet another amazing way the male and female bodies are designed to work together and benefit from each other.

Heart Health: As we've already learned, sex gets the heart pumping, which makes this vital life muscle stronger. But did you know that a strong heart enhances circulation and balances blood pressure? So, when a man has sex, he's actually being heart-smart and contributing to the fitness of the heart, a symbol of life and love.

As you can see, sex is so much more than a deed between two people. Any level of sexual activity has a positive effect on our overall health and well-being, and increasing evidence suggests that the more sex one has, the more benefits they receive. This is true not only for intercourse, but for masturbation, as well, because it produces the same release of hormones and substances that contribute to our life and longevity.

For this reason, I know that ED and PE are more than personal issues—they are valid health problems that require treatment. On multiple levels, they affect a man's ability to be as healthy and happy as he can be. That's why I'd like to reverse the trend to think of sex as a dirty deed that invokes secrecy and shame. It's a natural body function—our bodies are designed for it, positively enhanced by it, and strengthened through it. Every man deserves the opportunity to reap the rewards and benefits that a healthy, active, and fulfilling sex life brings to both him and his mate.

Chapter Ten

ED, PE, AND INFERTILITY

WHILE MY FOCUS IS not as a fertility specialist, my specialty does touch upon fertility. There are some common issues with infertility that cross over into erectile dysfunction and premature ejaculation. The main one being reduced self-esteem, but infertility introduces another emotion—inadequacy.

It's true that PE and ED are listed as reasons for infertility. But that doesn't mean that these men are sterile—just that they have a condition which interferes with their ability to deliver sperm deep into the vagina so conception can occur. Erectile dysfunction can be the underlying cause of infertility for men who cannot sustain an erection sufficient for intercourse. The same is true for premature ejaculation, when the male ejaculates prior to penetration. However, they are both treatable causes of infertility, so unless there are other fertility issues, like low sperm count, successful treatment of PE and ED might take care of the infertility issue.

I do want to correct any misunderstandings, though, that infertility and erectile dysfunction or premature ejaculation are one and the same. They are not. They are separate conditions. I believe that sometimes the words impotent and infertile are incorrectly interchanged and misused. A man can have PE or ED and still be very fertile, and often, he is. A male who is infertile (sterile) might not have any other sexual problems. A man should never automatically assume that because he has ED, he is infertile, because the odds are that he is very fertile. The same holds true for those who have short- or long-term premature ejaculation problems. The timing of their ejaculation is not a sign of infertility, but it could make impregnating a woman a bit more difficult.

The man who is both infertile and a premature ejaculator, though, receives a double whammy to his self-esteem. He develops a sense of inadequacy because he's not able to reproduce and satisfy his wife's maternal longings, and he feels inferior because he's not able to perform long enough to satisfy her sexually, too. In his own mind, he's beaten and defeated.

Virtually every man who suffers from ED or PE has a lack of self-esteem...which came first? The male's sexual problem or the emotion? My response is, either or both. I do know that ED and PE both cause a remarkable drop in a man's self-esteem, as does infertility. All three conditions can make a man feel like he's a disappointment—to himself and his wife.

Often, when I'm able to return a man's sexual confidence to him, he gets a tremendous boost to his self-esteem. He no longer feels inadequate or inferior, but takes pride in his ability to perform. If he's had fertility issues due to his inability to maintain an erection or prolong ejaculation, he now has an exciting new opportunity to remove the negative emotions and fears which result from both conditions. If his infertility is based on something else entirely, he can now explore options which might increase his sperm count or enhance his ability to father a child with a fertility specialist. By addressing the sexual problem, in many cases, we're able to simultaneously reduce the psychological and/or physical problems which result from it.

Chapter Eleven

WHEN A PARTNER ASKS, "WHAT CAN I DO TO HELP?"

SOME OF MY MALE patients have been known to bring their wives or partners to their first appointment. One such couple strikes my memory chord—they left such an impact on me that I'll never forget them. Married for decades, they were each in their 80's, devoted to each other and quite happy—except for the fact that the husband was suffering from ED. As a couple, they truly missed the sexual aspect of their relationship and openly admitted it. They both wanted it back and came to see me to rectify the problem.

One of the things that struck me about this couple was their age; but more important, I was impressed by the wife's support for her husband. If there was a problem, she was beside him all the way, doing whatever it took to find help and provide him with the love and support that she knew his self-esteem sorely needed.

While I am happy to report that this couple did regain their previously active sex life, I'm also happy to meet the women who are willing to openly communicate with and support their husbands. In doing so, they provide them with much-needed reassurance that they are loved and that they are willing to stick by their side, working on this, as in other things, together.

Men who don't have support from their wives are the ones who suffer from the highest feelings of inadequacy and depression. They fear not only the loss of their manhood, but also the potential loss of their mate. That's why, while normally I treat males, I'm including this section addressed to women, to let them know what they can do to help their husbands, give them reassurance, and boost their confidence.

Once in a while, I encounter patients who have well-meaning wives who reassure them that it doesn't matter if they aren't able to have sex anymore. While their intentions are good, these remarks and reassurances don't often achieve the desired result. One of the top concerns among my patients is that their wife doesn't understand— she doesn't get why it's a big deal for her husband to be able to achieve and maintain an erection. Reasoning that sex is just one aspect of their husband's life, a wife may remind him of his many other wonderful qualities and accomplishments. They're accomplished and good providers and great fathers. They've been successful in business and earned a name and reputation that should compensate for any other areas of lack in their lives. But I can tell you that it does not compensate in this area.

I've treated Wall Street tycoons, business owners, athletes, and men who have launched rockets. They're accomplished—but that doesn't override or even begin to compensate when things aren't working "down there." That's because a man's self-esteem cannot be overridden by a career or other successes. Even the most successful male is impacted by his ability, or inability, to achieve an erection. We are hardwired that way. It's important to these men that their wives understand the ingrained truth that an erection is part of their male identity and their psyche. Without it, they are bound to feel inadequate. Downplaying their husband's ED downplays the importance of who they are and what's important to them.

"My wife says it doesn't matter, but I know it does, and I feel like a failure." I've heard it time and time again. The last patient that stated this owned a multi-million dollar steel company...but he felt like a failure. More than anything, he needed his wife's support in understanding that, not a pat on the hand, telling him not to worry, it's okay. Because to him, it's definitely not okay.

Moreover, while I do treat men, it's worth noting that I understand that the women in their lives are also significantly impacted when their sex life is disrupted. Their point of view is important, too.

Gerald and Evelyn had an active sex life during their 30-year marriage. Then, Gerald had a sudden heart attack and underwent double by-pass surgery. It's been a year, and even though Gerald has received the all clear to resume sex, it hasn't happened. "I've tried, maybe too hard," said Evelyn. "It seems the more I tried to arouse him, the more pressure I created. Sure, I can tell that he's embarrassed, and he's apologized repeatedly, but I don't know what the problem is...Is it me? Or is it him? I simply don't know if I should be worried for him or our marriage. At this point, I'm frustrated, disappointed, and even a little angry. I've tried to be supportive, but as time goes on, Gerald won't even let me be affectionate toward him at all."

Evelyn is proof that men aren't the only ones who become disappointed when erectile dysfunction occurs. The problem this couple is facing is intensified by their reluctance to discuss it with each other. In silence, they're second guessing the reasons for their problem and each is shouldering a large portion of the blame. Talking about it respectfully and honestly would curb much of the stress and anxiety that they're having. Then, they could work together to find a treatment or solution that works. But first, they have to break the silence to find out if Gerald has a medical problem, a psychological fear that sex will induce another heart attack, or if his feelings for Evelyn have changed. The status quo, however, will create further physical and emotional distance between them, which could ultimately cause harm to their marriage.

Opening that discussion is easier said than done for some. Evelyn blames herself, believing that at the age of 52, she's not as attractive as she used to be. Gerald admits to himself that he loves his wife and longs for sex, but can't bring himself to admit to his wife that he's impotent. He silently lives with the feeling that he's now "half a man." To avoid further embarrassment, he's chosen to desexualize his wife. Now they both feel inadequate and the low self-esteem they're both suffering crosses into other parts of their marriage.

The loss of a sex life due to ED or PE creates intense feelings for both men and women. Some of those feelings are the same—some are different. It's helpful to identify those feelings so you can effectively communicate them to each other.

Impotence can create frustration in both parties. It can also cause self-blame and guilt. A woman might express disappointment, while a man might label his emotion as one of despair. Both parties can experience fear, as well, but the woman might have a fear of rejection, while her husband has very real fear of failure. They're both likely to fear the effects that impotence will have on their marriage, while they share a mutual grief over the loss of intimacy.

A FEMALE'S POINT OF VIEW

As a spouse or love interest, women are often nurturing. When their sex life comes to a standstill, their thoughts range from worry that something is physically wrong with their husband to worry that there is something wrong with herself—and more. Let's take a look at some of the common frustrations and concerns.

"I wonder if he might be sick...what if there's something medically wrong with him?"

Every man who is experiencing more than temporary or inconsistent impotence or premature ejaculation should see a doctor. Women who wonder if a medical problem might be responsible are correct. Most cases of erectile dysfunction are the result of physical, not psychological or emotional, conditions. Luckily, a large percentage of those are very treatable. If your husband is suffering from ED, I urge you to encourage him to schedule an appointment with a doctor for a thorough exam.

"Maybe he's no longer attracted to me and doesn't love me anymore."

While some people certainly do fall out of love and grow apart, erectile dysfunction is usually not the first sign of a waning relationship. If relationship problems are the reason for the loss of his desire, you would probably have noticed those problems, whether they were financial, emotional, or otherwise. Impotence usually isn't the result of a lack of affection, although some men will avoid affection altogether if they have a fear that they will be unable to perform.

"I wonder if he's having an affair."

This can be one of the first thoughts to cross a woman's mind, especially if sex stopped suddenly and abruptly. If her husband becomes emotionally distant, as well, it can lead to thoughts of betrayal. Openly discussing what's happening in your marriage and expressing your feelings will go a long way toward eliminating those doubts and avoiding the worry and destruction of trust brought on when one partner is concerned the other is unfaithful.

Impotence and infidelity are two separate entities which can affect a relationship. Because they both pertain to matters of intimacy, though, impotence can provoke thoughts of an affair. Finding out the real problem is paramount to putting those fears to rest.

"Maybe I'm not pleasing him. It seems the harder I try, the worse it gets."

Frustration and self-blame eat at the soul, and they eventually can cause deep resentment in a marriage. If you're touching him in a way that once pleased him, you can feel relatively assured that it's not you. He probably wants to respond as much as you want him to.

Remember, this is new and frightening territory for him, too. He doesn't know what to do to reverse it, so he can't tell you. He feels like a failure, and the more he's pressured to perform, the more stress and anxiety he'll encounter. Rather than working at it, let affection come naturally. Encourage him gently and let him know that you enjoy other sexual activities besides intercourse.

"I feel like he doesn't care about my feelings. He doesn't seem to want to get help or talk about it."

It's not that he doesn't care about you...it's the fact that he's not ready to admit that his inability to perform is anything more than a temporary phase that will go away on its own. Talking about it will require admission that there is a problem, so will seeking a diagnosis and treatment. Again, his male psyche is very fragile right now. The last thing he openly wants to admit to his wife is that he can't perform, so he might shrug it off or blame it on pressures at work. Be supportive, even if he is reluctant to talk initially. State your feelings, but don't use accusations. Take the time to let him know that you miss him and want to work together to restore the intimacy in your relationship.

A MALE'S POINT OF VIEW

Men and women do have different perceptions in many areas of life. Regardless of how often the average man thinks about sex on a daily basis, I can attest to the fact that men who are unable to have sex think about it even more. To them, their sexuality defines who they are and who they've become.

"Not being able to have sex with my wife is a sign of weakness. I feel like a total failure."

It's common for men to think impotence makes them a failure. Their entire life has centered around their masculinity—they've been molded to be the provider, in the workplace and the bedroom. The inability to provide intimate relations to his wife eats at his self-esteem until he has little left. He no longer sees himself as strong and virile, but as inept.

"What if I can't get it back? Will she stop loving me or seek another man who will give her what I can't?"

I've treated many men who have had this very real fear. I've even heard of some who were so afraid of losing their wife entirely that they've given her permission to find someone who can fulfill her sexual needs. When a man fears abandonment, he might find himself separating himself emotionally and physically as a way to prepare for potential loss. Unfortunately, many men suffer this fear in silence, not knowing that there is help for their condition that will put this worry at ease.

"I can't even hug my wife anymore because I'm afraid if I show her affection, she'll expect sex."

Affection and romantic gestures do often lead to foreplay, and eventually, to sex. This is true for both men and women. A woman could be thinking these same thoughts, wondering if any touch or loving gesture will be construed as a request for sex, placing additional pressure on her husband. Relationships are based on physical and emotional closeness, however. Intimacy, with or without sex, is a healthy sign of love and affection. It's also a good way to express your commitment to work through this together.

"In order to protect myself from my own internal pain and fear, our relationship has become platonic. I can't confide that to her. She'd never understand."

Sadly, in an attempt to spare themselves from embarrassment, shame, and despair, some men may opt to remove sexuality from their relationship altogether. By choosing to see their partner in a non-sexual manner, they can avoid the guilt and shame that their impotence causes. It's one manner of avoiding the issue. It's my hope that the communication lines can open up so intimate conversations can occur that will motivate both parties to seek intervention and treatment before this happens.

As in everything in life, the inability to satisfactorily perform spurs an emotional response and alters a man's behavior, especially toward his wife. Some men choose to distance themselves from the problem. Others might want to handle it differently, through denial or suffering in silence. Knowing these behaviors can be helpful.

THE SILENT TREATMENT

He doesn't want to talk about it. When you bring it up, he changes the subject or quickly dismisses it as nothing to worry about. He's protecting himself from having to admit that there is a problem. Avoidance of the subject provides him with a delay in accepting and admitting that he needs help.

TRANSFERRING BLAME

In an effort to protect his ego, he first seeks to find other causes for his problem. He might blame it on work or say he hasn't been feeling like himself. His excuse might be that he's tired or that you're not doing something right. Again, this is another way to avoid admitting that there is a problem.

AVOIDANCE

By avoiding situations that can lead to sex, he saves himself from potential embarrassment. The last thing he wants is to experience yet another failure in the bedroom. So, he might avoid the bedroom altogether, falling asleep on the couch while watching TV instead. Or, he might intentionally create tension in the relationship, especially if he sees signs that you're feeling amorous. In rare instances, he may go so far to avoid being placed in a sexual situation that he'll do things to appear less appealing in your eye. The intent is to spare himself from further shame and humiliation.

PERSONALITY CHANGES

Men handle the loss of sexual desire and potency problems differently. Most suffer from some loss of self-esteem. It's true that many show signs of depression. Others may throw themselves into their work or uncharacteristically relieve their anxiety through exercise. Some might drink more than usual or to excess. These are all real signs that he's suffering and should be strong incentives for the woman in his life to offer her support and help, while encouraging him to get treatment.

FINALLY, GETTING HELP

Approaching your husband about ED or PE can require tact. Depending on your level of communication and openness regarding the subject, you can be the motivating factor that drives him to seek help. The conversation may be easier if you keep a few points in mind:

- Don't blame or accuse.

- Don't approach the subject in bed or immediately after an inability to perform.

- Be sincere, letting him know that your relationship is very important to you and that you love him.

- Be positive.

- Tell him that you know it's difficult to talk about, but that you think it's necessary—you want to support him—you're in this together.

- Reinforce his masculinity and manhood.

- Don't act as if this is a crisis...if he's reluctant, placing too much importance and urgency on the issue could cause him to become defensive.

- Talk about your feelings; *I feel sad that we aren't able to talk about this* is often less accusatory than *Your refusal to talk about this is a problem.*

- Reinforce the fact that medical problems are often the reason for ED and that there is treatment available that does work; offer to accompany him, if it will make him more comfortable.

- Directly ask him how you can help.

- Do your homework and have information available to share with him, such as pamphlets or brochures about a discrete clinic and the various treatments possible; make sure you include statistics on the success rate and that with some treatments, most men get immediate results.

- Ask him for feedback, encourage him to share his feelings. When he does, listen without interrupting.

- Give him some time alone to think about what you've said and to read the information you've provided. Don't force the issue, but do let him know that you'll be there if and when he's ready to talk.

Gerald and Evelyn had this talk, and not only did it restore their sex life, it also saved their marriage. Gerald admitted that he was fearful of having another heart attack, but didn't know what to do about it. Evelyn had taken matters into her own hands and requested information on erectile dysfunction and the various treatments beforehand. With some gentle encouragement, she was able to convince Gerald to make an appointment. To Gerald's surprise, not only did his treatment work immediately, but it provided him with an erection despite his fears. With each instance of sex without a cardiovascular incident, he gained much-

needed confidence and reassurance in his ability to perform and please his wife.

Their other problems were exposed when the communication lines opened. Evelyn shared her feelings of inadequacy with her husband, who reassured her that she was still attractive and admitted that he had subconsciously stopped thinking of her as a sexual being to save himself from the fear of being a failure, in her eyes and his. Today, they happily report that they are both very satisfied with the frequency and quality of their sex life.

Chapter Twelve

DESPERATE TIMES CALL FOR DESPERATE MEASURES

AS A DOCTOR, IT'S enlightening to know about the products that claim to cure or treat ED. While I know what products really do work, I'm compelled to learn about all products, pharmaceutical or otherwise. Some piqué my interest, drawing me to research their claims and effectiveness. Yet others leave me either shaking my head or jaw dropped.

A man who can't "get it up" is often left with a feeling of sheer desperation. He'll do anything or try anything to regain his manhood, even resorting to some rather absurd measures. It appears, too, that there will always be someone somewhere who wants to capitalize on and advantage of his desperation, as evidenced by the products and procedures listed below.

Viagra® Beer: Yes, alcohol, the culprit that often is blamed for a man's inability to become erect, now claims to have the answer to a man's desire to enjoy a cold one without affecting his ability to perform. Viagra® beer was introduced in Britain in honor of the recent royal nuptials. It contains 7.5 percent alcohol, but its claim to fame isn't its alcohol content—it's the brewer's addition of male enhancement supplements. The fine print reveals that Viagra® isn't an ingredient at all, but it does contain horny goat weed, an herbal supplement, and other aphrodisiacs, like chocolate.

The beer's marketing efforts claim that slugging three beers will provide the drinker with the equivalent effect of taking one Viagra®. The appeal is that a guy can get a beer buzz and still get it up, but again, there are no regulations over what goes into the beer or the potential side effects.

Magic Power Coffee: While beer might be a guy's evening beverage of choice, coffee undoubtedly earns the morning spot. And what could be better than coffee that treats erectile dysfunction! Magic Power coffee is available on-line, and it joins the ranks of enhanced coffees that now claim to have benefits, like another new coffee product that states it helps people lose weight. According to this coffee, your morning brew can now help your morning erection because it contains ingredients which claim to increase blood flow to the penis. Sadly, like many such products, though, this coffee's supposed ability to increase endurance and stamina has triggered an FDA warning—there is no proof.

The FDA added another warning with this product. It contains herbal supplements (goji berry, horny goat weed, and ginseng) and a chemical ingredient similar to Viagra® that can pose health problems, the least of which is dizziness. Of great concern is its potential to reduce blood pressure to dangerously low levels and a risk of death. Coffee makers should stick to making a good cup of coffee, and let doctors stick to treating ED. It's fine to drink coffee to get your morning kick, but not if it kicks you back.

Reflexology: Reflexology is putting pressure on certain points of the body to affect another part. Most commonly, these pressure points are used to reduce pain and affect health. Now some reflexologists claim it's a natural cure for impotence. The problem with that assertion is that there is no proof that putting pressure on the foot will cause a man to become erect. However, I'll admit that it might have some effect for men who are aroused by being touched on the foot, but if that's all it took to achieve an erection, they probably wouldn't need reflexology, just a clean foot and a woman who doesn't mind a little foot foreplay.

Viagra® gum: What will they think of next? Gum laced with Viagra® now gives Wrigley's slogan of doubling your pleasure and doubling your fun new meaning. I don't know about most men and women, but I find it hard to believe that chomping on a wad of gum and blowing a bubble of Viagra®-enhanced gum is conducive to a great sex life. Besides that, you have to travel to Mexico to get a stick, which gives yet new meaning to another phrase—are you traveling for business or pleasure?

Penis pump: Now, I know men will go to a lot of extremes to become erect, but using a penile pump is an extreme measure. First, you place your penis in a tube and then you get the pleasure of vacuuming it to force the blood to flow into it. But you're not done yet. Once the blood is there and you become erect, you place an elastic band around your member to hold that erection. Somehow, this doesn't sound like fun. In fact, for many men it's painful and they become bruised. I can't imagine terrific sex after having to excuse yourself to pump up, having intercourse with a rubber band strapped to your penis, and having to pump back up when you become deflated. It should also be noted that the embarrassment of erectile dysfunction is only compounded when a man has to pull out a contraption such as this. Frankly, it shouldn't be this hard to get hard.

Desperate times do, indeed, call for desperate measures. Men who resort to downing beer and coffee, chewing gum, and getting a foot massage to fix their problems are grasping at straws. Those who subject themselves to the pain of pumps, or worse, penile implants, obviously don't know that there's a much easier, more effective, and less painful way to arouse their member. And until we can take the taboo out of men's sexual health, sadly, they might never know.

Chapter Thirteen

IS AN OUNCE OF PREVENTION WORTH A POUND OF CURE?

AN APPLE A DAY keeps the doctor away, or so the saying goes. But when the concept pertains to erectile dysfunction, are there any tried and true ways to prevent it from happening to you? Because we already know that a man's erection, or lack of one, is often indicative of his overall health and well being, it's likely that a program to improve his health could positively impact and improve his sexual health, as well. Let's take a look at some of the things that men can do to prevent erectile dysfunction and premature ejaculation.

Exercise. You might dread the word, but exercise truly does benefit all parts of the body, even the penis. No, it doesn't make the penis muscular, but exercise does get the heart and blood pumping, something every erection requires. How much exercise do you need? Every little bit helps. Taking a half hour walk a few days a week has proven to be effective in minimizing incidences of ED. Any cardio workout will help, whether it's running, walking, playing tennis, swimming, weight training, or team sports. A good rule of thumb to follow is, if it will help your heart, it can help your love life.

What about penis exercises? Known as pelvic or Kegel exercises, this form of exercise is suggested to strengthen the muscles that control a man's ejaculation and urine stream. They can help a man who is recovering from prostate problems or surgery, or the man who suffers from occasional premature ejaculation. However, there isn't any solid evidence that these exercises have any significant or long-term impact on a man's erection or ability to perform.

Reduce stress and anxiety. If there is one thing that I know is effective in preventing ED and PE, it's reducing the stress factor. Men naturally impose a standard of performance on themselves, which causes a certain amount of pressure or anxiety to meet that standard. The pressure to perform is psychological, but it manifests itself in physical ways.

The stress, anxiety, and pressure not only are the root of some men's problems, but they're also guilty of making the problem worse. It's similar to "which came first, the chicken or the egg?" Does this stress and anxiety cause ED and PE, or does it make it more difficult to overcome ED and PE? I say both. Therefore, do yourself a favor—don't be so hard on yourself. Reduce your expectations a bit. Nobody said you have to be a sexual superhero to enjoy sex. Be realistic, take deep breaths, calm down, and enjoy the moment. Your body will respond.

Control your environment. Whether you need to reduce interruptions or create a more seductive atmosphere, the environment will affect your ability to perform. If you're bored, your penis will be, too. If you're stimulated, well, then that's good news. Determine the atmosphere that is conducive to your desires and create it.

That environment is about more than squeaky bed springs and creating a seductive atmosphere, though. It's also includes an emotional atmosphere. While it's true that some men have difficulty performing under pressure, studies have also shown that some men can't perform if they sense sadness. Sexual chemistry is real. The ability to become erect is dependent on the stimulation of our senses—sight, sound, taste, touch and smell. Sadness is an emotional bummer, for sure, but did you know that men who smell a woman's tears lose their sexual desire? I'm not referring to seeing a woman cry or consoling her, but the mere smell of a woman's tears when she's sad.

The chemical compound in a woman's tears lowers a man's testosterone level, as well as his heart rate and respiration, as well as the brain activity that signals arousal. So the next time your lady wants to watch a sad movie, don't smell her tears!

Sleep. The amount and quality of sleep we get does more than re-energize our bodies and enhance our mood, it also is a factor in our risk for urinary tract disorders, one of which is erectile dysfunction. Two recent studies have shown that middle-aged men (averaging 47 years of age) who had incidences of sleep deprivation, poor quality of sleep, and/or sleep apnea are at an increased risk of having urinary tract problems in the future. Furthermore, it was also found that the men who suffered from erectile dysfunction are twice as likely to have sleep apnea—the more severe the ED, the more likely they were to have obstructive sleep apnea. This is proof that there is a stronger correlation between the bedroom and sex than just the bed. The ability to get a good night's sleep on a regular basis is conducive to our overall health and our ability to perform. So sleep can be more than an effective way of preventing a trip to the urologist or a visit to a sleep apnea clinic; eight hours of sleep a day just might keep ED away.

Erectile dysfunction and premature ejaculation cannot always be prevented, though. It's important to understand that. But it's also important to know that men can prevent these conditions from totally sabotaging their sex life by being a little bit more self-forgiving. Remember, erectile dysfunction and premature ejaculation happen to most men at some point in their life. Don't dwell on it and don't place additional pressure on yourself or you'll only make the cycle spin faster.

Lastly, I want to state that the best prevention for ED and PE is to know your body. Pay attention to the regularity of your erections and what might be happening in your life and in your health to affect them. Take care of yourself, and your sex life will benefit, as well. And know that if you are having problems, it's a sign that something is going on behind the scenes that's affecting your ability to perform. If that happens, don't let it be the beginning of your journey of grief over what you've lost, but let it be a sign that you need the help of a professional who can and will help you recapture it, because while there may not be any method of prevention that's one hundred percent effective, there are treatments with a success just as high.

THE SOLUTION

Chapter Fourteen

AN ERECTION FOR ANY MAN, REGARDLESS...

I SUBTITLED THIS BOOK *Any Man, Regardless of His Age or Medical History, Can Still Get an Erection* because my experience proves that to be true. Yet, time and again, my experience also continues to prove that most men believe that I mean any man...*except him.* For some reason, they believe they are exempt from successful treatment, most likely because they are afraid to get their hopes up. By the time they come to my office, many of my patients have tried so many other unsuccessful methods and treatments that they are admittedly and justifiably disillusioned.

The first thing I tell them is that they are not exempt—they *can* get an erection. They can enjoy a healthy, active sex life, whether they are 21 or 91 years old. Yet, the old cliché still lives...they've got to see it to believe it.

I get to see something, too. I get to see their surprise and then their unbridled joy in knowing that their manhood is not dead, but rather alive and well. I get to see the transformation that successful treatment brings—an increase in their self-esteem and confidence. It's almost as if I can see the heavy weight they've been carrying suddenly melt away. Believe me, the rewards are immense, and they never fail to move me.

That's why I chose this specialty, as unusual as it is. Yes, it's rare for a physician to choose to specialize in treating ED and PE, which is unfortunate because there are many men across the country who desperately need the treatment we offer.

That treatment is different for every man—but for every man there is a successful treatment—even when it appears that there is no hope. One of my associates told me of such a case—a patient we'll never forget.

I sat down with a 24 year old patient, who was paralyzed from the chest down. He was, unfortunately, a victim of a hate crime—gang related—from college. Since his graduation from college, he has since found a young lady that he wanted to marry and start a family with. Unfortunately, because of his injury, he was unable to achieve an erection of any sort.

The patient had been told by his doctors that he would NEVER be able to use this part of his body ever again, and that he would never be able to have sex again with his partner, nor start a family of his own. He told us he was completely devastated that this had happened to him, and that he feared he was slipping into a depressive state.

The medication that we custom-blended for this patient gave him the opportunity to achieve and maintain an erection to its fullest. He was floored that we were able to help him achieve what he had been told was impossible.

That young man is just one of the many reasons I love my job. Not only were we able to help him achieve an erection, but we were able to open the door for him to have a wife and a family.

By treating a man, we also get to make a positive influence on his relationships. It's true that ED and PE impact both partners, which is why I dedicated a portion of this book to wives and partners and how they can help. Sexual activity and intimacy are natural ways to express love and desire—without it, relationships suffer. The next story, again told to me, reveals just how important sex is to relationships.

I personally treated a patient that was on his last chance of hope in correcting this problem. To the point he was in tears, he asked me and Dr. Hornsby for the best help we could give him. His relationship was on the brink of disaster because of his lack of performance, and we received the opportunity to fix that for him. He had suffered with this problem for nearly 15 years, and within an hour of visiting us, he received the response to our medication for treating ED he had been seeking for all those years.

His wife immediately demanded to see Dr. Hornsby. (I was scared at first because I thought I had done something wrong!) I went to Dr. Hornsby, and he agreed to come back to the room where the patient and wife were sitting. Before he could even get in the room completely, the patient's wife got up and hugged Dr. Hornsby's neck, and she kept saying, "Thank You! Thanks so much!" It was a moving experience.

In both of these instances, we were able to help men not only achieve an erection for the first time in a long time, but we were able to help their relationships. Obviously, the treatments we provide are of immense benefit to both partners.

The same treatment we provided those two patients can help you, too. You are *not* exempt when I say *any* man can have an erection. You can have an erection. You can have an active and healthy sex life starting the very day you walk through our doors. I know, because I've had the pleasure of helping thousands of men who thought there was no hope. It's why I love my job—I get to help people every single day. I get to give men (and their partners) new beginnings and happy endings. I get to play a small part in changing somebody's life in a big way. And I can help you, because I know that ANY man, *regardless of his age or medical history,* CAN still get an erection.

ABOUT DR. KEVIN HORNSBY

KEVIN HORNSBY M.D. initially attended Enterprise State Junior College in Enterprise, AL, where he was later uniquely recognized as the Alumnus of the Year for his achievements. He completed a Bachelors of Science degree in Zoology at Auburn University, in Auburn, Alabama, and continued with coursework toward a Masters degree in Physiology, while completing required courses for medical school.

He was a first-year applicant acceptance to the University of Alabama School of Medicine, where he was recognized as one of only 40 medical students annually who were awarded scholarships to the Betty Ford Clinic to study addiction disease. Dr. Hornsby was named Senior Class President of his medical school class, affirming his leadership and acceptance from his peers in advanced medical training.

Entering a family practice residency at UAB in the mid-nineties, Dr. Hornsby was positioned at the right place and right time to see the beginnings and development of many of the modern treatments of erectile dysfunction that are used today. As a resident spending multiple rotations in Urology under the supervision and training of Keith Lloyd, M.D., and Anton Bueschen, M.D., at UAB, Dr. Hornsby was given an early window into new trials, evaluations, and unique treatments explored and used to treat study patients in the UAB Erectile Dysfunction Clinic at University Hospital in Birmingham, AL.

Dr. Hornsby was once again honored for his leadership abilities at the end of his training when he was appointed to be chief resident in his final year of residency training. Today, he is the medical director of clinics devoted to the specific treatment of ED and PE. He is a member of the Sexual Medicine Society of North America and The International Society of Sexual Medicine, attending frequent medical meetings on the latest advancements in sexual medicine and dysfunction. To date, Dr. Hornsby has successfully treated well in excess of 10,000 men for erectile dysfunction using various methodologies – some not well known to the general public.

To learn more or to contact Dr. Kevin Hornsby, please visit www.drhornsbymd.com, or contact Men's Medical Clinics National Headquarters, 5728 Major Blvd., Suite 750, Orlando, Florida 32819 (407) 730-8500 or (800) 329-7310.